Crossing the

Representations of Deaf

RACHEL M. HARTIG

Gallaudet University Press
Washington, DC

Gallaudet University Press
Washington, DC
http://gupress.gallaudet.edu

Library of Congress Cataloging-in-Publication Data

Hartig, Rachel Mildred.
  Crossing the divide : representations of deafness in biography / Rachel M. Hartig.
     p. cm.
  Includes bibliographical references and index.
  ISBN 1-56368-298-2 (alk. paper)
    1. Deaf—History. 2. Deaf—Biography. 3. Biographers—Biography. 4. Berthier, Jean-Ferdinand, 1803-1886. 5. Pitrois, Yvonne. 6. Rocheleau-Rouleau, Corinne, 1881–1963. 1. Title.
  HV2370.H37 2006
  362.4′20922—dc22   2006015909

Contents

Preface

IN THEIR groundbreaking work *Deaf in America: Voices from a Culture*, Padden and Humphries discuss how "battling against lives proposed by others" (110) is a central theme in the lives of deaf people in American society. For deaf people, integration into the world of others too often meant enforced oralism and the denial of American Sign Language (ASL) and the culture that it defined and expressed.

The strong belief that deaf people must create their own lives had, as early as 1856, led John James Flournoy, a deaf Georgian, to make the radical proposal that deaf people establish their own state in the West. Separateness was necessary for the special needs of the deaf to be met, he asserted. A spirited dialogue, through letters, followed in the *American Annals for the Deaf and Dumb* (1856–1858), where the extreme nature of Flournoy's position was ridiculed. His proposal seemed to ignore the reality that many families had both deaf and hearing children, not to mention the obvious financial barriers to the establishment of such a state. Nonetheless, he had seen the profound need for deaf people to maintain their own language and culture, a need as real and important today as it was in 1856.

Although articulated for and about the American deaf community, this issue is one central to the French deaf community as well. French Sign Language (LSF) is now used in most French schools for the deaf, it is true, but French deaf people still feel a pressing need to associate in community and to articulate their identity and their needs. Their development had been impeded by the 1880 World Conference for the Deaf in Milan. At that conference, the Abbé de l'Épée's legacy was refuted. Throughout Europe, oralism was restored and sign language was forbidden as a means of educating deaf children.

Diversity has been a popular concept in Europe and America for several decades now. Most of us recognize the profound value that each culture within our larger culture brings to us: beyond the gifts of linguistic variety, there are important challenges to our thinking about literature, politics, and ethics. But at what point does an individual's assimilation into society endanger his sense of personal identity?

The three subjects of this work, the French biographers Jean-Ferdinand Berthier (1803–1886) and Yvonne Pitrois and the Franco-American biographer Corinne Rocheleau (1881–1963), offer interesting individual responses to this dilemma, and their work deserves to be read not only for their insights but also because they are, all three, fine biographers with a commitment to chronicling the stories of the deaf individuals of their era and the communities to which they belonged.

All three shared a passion for narrating lives, and all three used the genre of biography not only as a way to record and commemorate others' lives, but also as a way to explore their own innermost selves and to deal with feelings of ambivalence about their own deafness. They differed, however, in the manner in which they crossed the cultural divide between the deaf and the hearing. For Berthier, it was through his social and political activism and his scholarship. Pitrois was dedicated to learning and telling the stories of the deaf and the deaf-blind with a moral end in view, and Rocheleau presented a radiant feminism, inclusive of both deaf and hearing women.

Are these different approaches to crossing the cultural divide as valid today as they were at the time that the authors made their intellectual and moral choices? These biographers and their subjects remind both hearing and deaf readers that it is possible to be respectful of our unique heritages while, at the same time, participating in our larger society and making substantial contributions to it. The right balance is hard to achieve, however, and this book traces the efforts of three biographers who managed successfully, but at significant personal cost, to transcend marginalization and stigma to arrive at both an acceptance of self and other. Can we hope for better than that in these early years of the twenty-first century?

Knowing, in fact, how much these writers have to offer us today, both in terms of their ideas and their artistry, it has been hard for me to finish this volume with so many questions left unanswered. What were Berthier's last years like? Did he write any formal reply to the decrees of the Congress of Milan? Did Yvonne Pitrois and Helen Keller ever meet face to face? Did the very private Pitrois ever yield to a desire to write a biographical statement that might have told us more about her personal, as opposed to her professional, life? These authors have become friendly ghosts during the course of my research for the book and they deserve better than to be portrayed in an incomplete way.

I am grateful to the many friends who have urged me to present this volume and to see it as the beginning of a dialogue with others fascinated by deaf history. I do so with the hope that colleagues will pick up the trail and add to the dialogue, possibly answering some of the questions I have asked, and asking and answering many of their own. It has been a great adventure trying to pull together such elusive material and equally exciting trying to interpret it. And though I would have preferred to offer more complete narratives of the lives of my three biographers, the thoughtfulness of their choices and the value of their work remains apparent.

Acknowledgments

THIS BOOK, both in its conception and realization, owes so much to so many friends and colleagues. My particular thanks to Vic Van Cleve and Ivey Pittle Wallace of Gallaudet University Press. Vic helped me to formulate the project and Ivey to present my ideas in the clearest possible way. Both were a constant source of encouragement and support.

Thanks, as well, to my excellent colleagues at the Gallaudet Research Institute, Michael Karchmer, Len Kelly and Tom Allen, dean of the Graduate School, who not only provided me with the financial support to travel to archives in this country and abroad but also offered helpful critiques of sections of the project while it was in its early stages.

Friends both on and off Gallaudet's campus were equally helpful. Mark Weinberg and Denise West offered excellent technical support and were remarkably patient as I struggled to familiarize myself with a new computer and printer. Ellen Loughran kindly loaned me a book from her mother's library that aided in the formulation of chapter 1, and Jerry Komisar and Anne Quartararo gave excellent suggestions on the Berthier chapter. Rose and Joe Krieger, Janice Mitchell, Gordon Kirschner, and George Satran were wonderful listeners anytime I needed to discuss a new idea or concern, and my cousin Herbert Stone reminded me of the existence of the Helen Keller library in Manhattan.

Thanks, as well, to Monica Berger and the successive librarians at the American Foundation for the Blind library in New York City for materials on the Helen Keller–Yvonne Pitrois connection and to the Sisters of Providence in Montreal, Canada, for so kindly mailing me the materials from their archives that chronicled Corinne Richelieu's years there both as a student and as an educator.

Finally, I would like to extend my appreciation to my incomparable friends abroad. Alexis Karacostas first let me walk through the Deaf

Archives at the Institut National de Jeunes Sourds, enabling me to make my earliest discoveries there. My friend Michelle Balle-Stinckwich, their current archivist, provided me with a wealth of resources on the major authors discussed in my work and was always ready with a creative new approach and helpful suggestions. Yves Delaporte was aware of my fascination with Yvonne Pitrois and took the time and trouble to mail me any relevant articles he came across as he pursued his own research.

All of these talented people made it possible for me to complete the book. I can only hope that it adequately reflects the generous assistance that all of them provided. The author expresses her heartfelt gratitude to them all.

Crossing the Divide

1 On the Nature of Biographical Form

Is Biography Disguised Autobiography?

MODERN BIOGRAPHY is marked by the spirit of free inquiry. As readers, we do not expect biographers to allow preconceived ideas to dictate judgments. We expect them to be guided by the facts, unimpeded by either admiration or hostility. This differs from an earlier era when a biographer might write uncritically about a friend or family member, offering praise or at least withholding information that would be unflattering to the subject. Today's biographers are held to a different standard. They must not alter historical truth, and while aspiring to a standard of objectivity, biographers must have some "sympathy of feeling" for and with their subjects.[1]

Noted twentieth-century biographers André Maurois and Leon Edel stressed that biography must reveal the individual within history. According to Edel, "No lives are led outside history or society; they take place in human time."[2] Nevertheless, because human beings are at the heart of the biographical enterprise, historical events must revolve around them, serving as a background for, or intersecting with, each life and often providing a rationale for the subject's choices and actions.

This volume explores the efforts of three French deaf biographers of the nineteenth and twentieth centuries to find themselves as individuals and as artists and to bridge the cultural divide between deaf and hearing people by means of their biographical studies of others. All of the authors included took seriously the historical dimension of their work, but they recognized the centrality of their protagonists. Jean-Ferdinand Berthier (1803–1886) always sketched the history, particularly the political history, that encircled his protagonists. He wrote not only of politics within the Paris Institute for the Deaf, which was the setting for most of his work, but of the politics in France that similarly impacted his protagonists. Thus in the 1839 study entitled *Notice sur la Vie et les Ouvrages d'Auguste Bébian* (*Notice on the Life and Works of Auguste Bébian*), Berthier relates that Bébian was fired from the institute because his spirit of rebellion angered those in power in the school administration. Berthier's lengthy 1873 analysis of Abbé Sicard, the second director of the institute, recounts Sicard's arrest in 1792 as a counterrevolutionary and his close brush with the guillotine. These dramatic circumstances notwithstanding, it was the lives-in-full of the two men that Berthier portrayed and that hold the attention of the reader.

Yvonne Pitrois's portrait of Helen Keller, *Une nuit rayonnante: Helen Keller* (*A Shining Night: Helen Keller*), placed Keller in the context of other deaf-blind people whose lives preceded hers, that of Laura Bridgman in particular. But it was the destiny of Helen Keller and her unique relationship with her teacher Anne Sullivan that was the focus of Pitrois's study. Corinne Rocheleau recounted the historical circumstances that led French-Canadian pioneer women to leave France, but the true value of her work, *Françaises d'Amérique* (*Heroic French Women of Canada*, 1915), is found in the portraits that she wrote of the pioneer women. She depicted them as individuals, reflecting a broad spectrum of female personalities and activities: maternal women, warriors, religious women, and the emphasis was clearly on their lives and the choices they made.

Thus, in spite of the importance of the historical aspects of each biography, the biographer must be more than a historian. The biographer must remain focused on the portrayal of the development of a single life. "Biography is the study of the evolution of a human soul,"[3] according to Maurois, so it is particularly important for the biographer to discover and portray the moments when the subject became himself, found a vocation, overcame weaknesses, and developed a new understanding of life. Berthier's biography of the Abbé de l'Épée (1852) sketches the moment when L'Épée discovered his vocation—he stumbled on two deaf girls in a house on Fossés-St. Victor Street, recognized their vulnerability because of their disability, and decided to devote his life to teaching them and others like them. Helen Keller made a trope toward goodness once she was able to communicate, and this development is at the heart of Yvonne Pitrois's analysis of her. Rocheleau's study of Ludivine Lachance in *Hors de sa prison* (*Out of Her Prison*, 1927), showed the touching development of strength on the part of her deaf-blind heroine. Terrified of death when it was first explained to her, Ludivine ultimately accepted her own death with courage when her time came. For all three writers, then, it was clearly the development of character that was at the heart of the narrative.

All biographers are on a quest for the truth. They must consider which materials can be used to find and to record the truth about their subjects. They must see what others have written about a chosen subject and read letters, diaries, and journals written by the subject. But even after such careful research, the biographer must be aware that the subject may be posing and that the words of others may be contradictory. The biographer must cultivate "faculties of artistic divination," as well as scientific investigation, in order to be successful in finding and portraying the subject with accuracy.[4]

Further complicating this quest is an understanding on the part of modern biographers of the complexities of personality. Berthier, Pitrois, and Rocheleau all understood that the quest for the truth includes an acknowledgment of the protagonist's faults as well as his virtues. Berthier, although he deeply admired the Abbé de l'Épée, wrote that L'Épée did not always have sufficient faith in the possibilities of sign language in and of itself, without alteration. In this same analysis, Berthier acknowledged the abbé's commitment to the children he taught, even depriving himself of heat in the hard winter of 1788, in order to save the kindling for his young students. Similarly, Pitrois underlined the brilliance and dedication to social service for the blind and deaf-blind of Helen Keller, while faulting her for her vaudeville appearances with Anne Sullivan. Pitrois saw these performances as undignified and sensationalistic, an interesting view that will be discussed in depth in a later chapter. Rocheleau, in her portrait of Jeanne le Ber in *Françaises d'Amérique* . . . , showed us a "saintly recluse" who desired to live following the laws of God but failed in her earthly commitments to family and friends.

CAN AUTOBIOGRAPHICAL narrative provide us with the truth more readily than biography? It would seem so, as who better than the man himself to write about his own motives or the secrets behind his actions? But numerous factors make even autobiographical narratives false. We forget a lot about our own lives, a phenomenon that occurs throughout our lives and that may have numerous causes. There may be aesthetic reasons, as an autobiographer may be tempted to make of his life a work of art, often eliminating, without realizing it, the everyday events that reveal what that person had in common with others. This might create the impression that his life was more different than it really was. Forgetfulness might also be triggered by the censorship the mind performs upon the disagreeable or the shameful. We may want to forget humble origins or embarrassing episodes in our lives. Memory often fails through a process of rationalization. An event may be the work of chance, but we may discover, in retrospect, a heroic narrative.

Additional obstacles to creating authentic autobiographies and memoirs exist for people with disabilities, deaf people, women, and other marginal groups. This genre was long defined by men in the mainstream of society. The powerful early writers of autobiography, Augustine and Rousseau, do not offer adequate models for writers on the margins of society. Perhaps in some measure due to an absence of models, none of the deaf authors included in this analysis wrote a full-length autobiography. Writing, in general, before autobiographies were too much in fashion and perhaps additionally distanced from this form by his marginality, Berthier did not even write a memoir. He did include personal observations and comments in his biographies of deaf educators. His affection for Laurent Clerc and his continuing correspondence and relationship with him long after Clerc's initial departure from France are revealed in an essay appended to the biography of the Abbé Sicard.

Pitrois included moral observations that reflected her religious views in her biographies, but she left neither memoirs nor autobiographical essays. Some rich comments, however, surface in her newsletter for deaf people, *La Petite Silencieuse* (*The Little Silent Girl*).[5] There we learn of her close relationship with her mother and of her deep concern for deaf and deaf-blind people. Pitrois used the newsletter to urge her readers to support one another and to collect books, clothing, and money from those able to spare it for the benefit of the poorest. It is perhaps this same religiosity and moral rigor that prevented her from chronicling herself—this, coupled with the fact that it was still considered inappropriate for women to write about themselves and their personal aspirations.

Rocheleau, alone of the three, wrote an autobiographical essay, "My Education in a Convent School for the Deaf," in 1931. It is a partial analysis, covering only the years up to and including the oralist education she received at the convent school in Montreal. The essay narrates the devastation Rocheleau felt upon becoming deaf at the age of nine and how her studies at this school, after many failed attempts to find a suitable education, finally enabled her to reconnect with family and friends and lead a productive life. The essay is sensitively written and reflects a courage and assertion that this disabled woman's life is worth the retelling. Rocheleau revealed herself here as an early feminist, an aspect of her work and life that will be analyzed more completely in a later chapter. Her essay resembles more modern biographical writing in that she does not write about a completed life but about a life in progress, and the writing itself becomes part of her process of defining herself.

Maurois asserted that autobiography, like biography, is difficult to create. We need appropriate models. We cannot completely retrieve the past, as it is impossible not to change it both consciously and unconsciously. He believed that an intellectual autobiography is the closest one can come to writing an authentic autobiography. Such a biography, he said, recounts how a person's intelligence and ideas were developed. His belief was that, in this manner, there are fewer subjective or emotional elements that come into play.[6] Rocheleau approached this model in her essay, which focused in large measure on her educational development both before and during her years in the convent school.

As works with both historical and scientific dimensions, the best biographies and autobiographies must be works of art, as well. The first and most important choice of the biographer is that of his subject. The biographer must then uncover what is unique about the protagonist. Although the life depicted may manifest the influence of some underlying philosophy, the author must avoid being heavy-handed in the expression of that philosophy. To achieve artistic effect, he may, instead, analyze the themes and motifs that reveal a hidden artistic unity.

How else can the biographer respect scientific truth but still approach the art of the novelist? First, he must follow chronological order, allowing for the portrayal of the evolution of the human spirit in the individual. Character evolves in contact with human beings and events. These influences revealed in their progression will ideally lead to art, which depends upon a sense of movement. Thus, even though the characters of a biography or autobiography are real, they may still be appropriate material for a work of art, if the biographer composes his work with care.

Midway between art and science, reflecting elements of both, are the findings of Sigmund Freud and his successors, and their influence on biography. There was, after Freud, a new arena for biographical study. Reading audiences wanted to know more about human nature and the motivations for human achievement. There was a desire to learn about the inner life, as well as the outer life, of the subject. The biographer had to pay heed to this in his "recording and telling of human lives."[7] A new form of biography called "psychobiography" developed, essentially beginning with Lytton Strachey, who was the first to use Freud in a creative way in his work. The biographer now was expected to discover and understand his subject's secrets and feelings, as well as how the subject handled his or her own life.

The biographer also needed to understand himself, his own inner life, well enough so that he didn't confuse it with that of his subject. *Transference* is the term used to describe the involvement between psychoanalyst and patient that occurs during psychiatry. It is the development of an emotional attitude toward the analyst on the part of a patient, which may be either positive or negative. By seeing these attachment patterns and interpreting them, the analyst gains understanding. (Edel believed that, in fact, the analyst may be considered a biographer of the soul.) Biographers have a similar emotional attachment to their subjects but often don't acknowledge it or understand it completely.

How do biographers choose their subjects? According to Edel, Freud observed in his study of Leonardo da Vinci that biographers became quite obsessed with their heroes.[8] The biographer's choice of subject may be a response to some hidden need in his own personality or nature. At the heart of the biographical enterprise is "the relation of the biographer to the subject."[9] In *Aspects of Biography* (1929), André Maurois, without specifically using the term *transference*, described his relationship with his own biographical subjects in exactly those terms. He added that when the author chooses his subject in response to a personal need, biography can be said to be disguised autobiography. Similarly, according to Edel in *Writing Lives* (1984), Vladimir Nabokov felt that all biographers were individuals who completed their lives by writing the lives of others.

A biographer, then, may use his writing to work through his own personal obsessions, or he may portray in his work what life has denied him, depicting the subject as the kind of man he would himself hoped to become. He may, like the novelist Marcel Proust who translated his illnesses and withdrew from life's difficulties into the rich world of Combray, convert negatives into positives, revealing "the triumphs of art over neuroses and of literature over life."[10] We return, then, to Maurois's theory, supported by Edel, that biography is disguised autobiography.

All three of the deaf biographers featured in this volume used the biographical form to help themselves to understand, to heal, and to resolve feelings about their deafness at a safer distance than autobiographical confession would have allowed. Their subjects, in large measure, wrestled with issues similar to those experienced by the authors, or found a way to transcend them.

Awakened to the vulnerable situation of deaf people in society by his loss of standing at the National Institute for the Deaf in Paris between 1832 and 1836, Berthier portrayed, in all of his studies, the political pressures that influenced the lives of his subjects, as they had his own. Through his writing, Berthier was able to learn from his successive subjects and moderate his own anger and frustration. The healing effects of writing about his own issues, through the more comfortable medium of biographical sketches of others, led to an effective catharsis that enabled him to live his own life more creatively.

The trauma that Pitrois would try to resolve through her biographies was her loss of hearing and vision, as a result of sunstroke, at the age of seven. Between the ages of seven and twelve, Pitrois struggled between light and darkness, finally regaining her vision, although she remained deaf all her life. Even though she recovered her sight, Pitrois was deeply affected by the temporary experience of its loss, and her biographies reflect this preoccupation. Her biography of Helen Keller and the trilogy of biographies entitled *Trois lumières dans la nuit: Valentin Haüy, Louis Braille, Maurice de la Sizeranne* (*Three Lights in the Darkness: Valentin Haüy, Louis Braille, Maurice de la Sizeranne*) allowed her to explore heroes who benefited the blind community and, in the cases of Keller, Braille, and de la Sizeranne, were blind themselves and therefore overcame great odds, including the inclination to become bitter. Through her exploration and analysis of these models, Pitrois would finally be able to defuse the haunting memory of her blindness.

Corinne Rocheleau chose to portray subjects who reflected her dual concerns for the place of deaf citizens and women in society. Her deafness at the age of nine had isolated her, but the education that she received at the convent school in Montreal gave her the tools, not only to survive, but to thrive. At the convent school, as well, she saw the nuns' dedication to their work, a dedication that Rocheleau wanted to emulate, and after observing the effectiveness of many of the sisters in their professional roles, she came to believe that a woman could be scholar, teacher, and writer.

Rocheleau's writing would build on this foundation and additionally free her. In *Françaises d'Amérique*, she presented a panorama of women, all of whom lived in the New World but who made very different life choices. *Hors de sa prison* and *Those in the Dark Silence* (1930), dealing with deaf-blind subjects, enable her to resolve some of her remaining feelings of bitterness about her deafness. Rocheleau, in later years, served the deaf community extensively, as a writer and as a teacher. Her writing had sufficiently helped to defuse the negative feelings and to allow her to lead a creative, happier life and to make peace with her difference.

This element of emotion in psychobiography, however, must not keep the biographer's art from being objective. Although it is hard to avoid excessive emotional involvement with the material, the biographer needs to stand back and strive to be a "participant-observer."[11] There must be some involvement on the part of the biographer, but she should resist being taken over by her subject. The biographer must be sympathetic, yet sufficiently distant, both involved and uninvolved, and must be able to separate from the subject, according to Edel.

Berthier, Pitrois, and Rocheleau tended to involve themselves in their texts more than later biographers would find acceptable. They register moral approval or disapproval and clearly indicate whether they accept or reject their subjects' positions. All three, however, were impeccable in their research; they consulted works and letters in archives, and they interviewed surviving friends and colleagues who were contemporaries of their heroes. The reader can feel confident of their research, if not always of their interpretations.

For them, as well as for mainstream biographers, the major task of the biographer is to recover the mind of the subject. The text must be true to the human sources from which it springs, and therefore, the chronicler must take into account written archival materials and the application of psychoanalytical concepts of life writing when depicting the hero. The biographer must get beyond the appearance of things and establish a nuanced relationship with his or her subject that allows for an understanding of how the subject may have been motivated by compulsions, emotions, and passions to make significant life choices and how she fulfilled her destiny, or failed to do so.

The reader also has a relationship with the text and its hero. "The biographer makes himself like his hero in order to understand him; the reader in order to copy his actions."[12] A reader may be comforted, or may aspire to act more responsibly and become a more empathic person. Biography offers us lessons in morality by giving us a panorama of individual examples and reminding us that human beings have both positive and negative features and that we would do well to imitate the best, rather than the worst, examples. Challenges, then, exist for the reader, as they do for the biographer.

But regardless of its challenges, biography merits the doing, as the need for the hero is "as old as mankind."[13] It sets before us lofty but accessible, astonishing but credible, examples to follow. It seems to flourish particularly during periods of doubt and despair, appearing as a source of reassurance that people are capable of strength and goodness. It is a complex art form, and we demand much of it and its practitioners: "We demand of it the scrupulosity of science and the enchantments of art, the perceptible truth of the novel and the learned falsehoods of history."[14] But it meets our expectations, if not always on an individual basis, as a genre, by offering us heroes whose actions and voices sometimes uplift us and always interest and educate us to human potential.

THE HUMAN need for heroes exists just as strongly for people with disabilities who, until recently, lacked heroes and a voice. Thomas Couser believes that life-writing genres are particularly useful. But disability and illness narratives present particular challenges to a genre that, as we have seen, is already quite complex. The issues that Couser seeks to explore include how such narratives get written at all, given the disadvantaged position of the protagonists; and how can one make a coherent narrative out of such lives.[15]

Couser especially laments the rareness of deaf biography and autobiography. Although the study of marginalization with regard to race, class, gender, and sexual orientation has become quite prevalent, illness and disability studies have been slow to develop. Yet, as Couser asserts, this is the most widespread kind of marginalization.

He rightly points, however, to great progress in making the deaf community and its issues more visible, beginning with a deaf Renaissance initiated by William Stokoe's 1960 *Sign Language Structure*. Stokoe's research legitimated American Sign Language and the Deaf Pride and Deaf Empowerment movements in the 1970s that culminated in the Deaf President Now uprising at Gallaudet University in 1988 and the installation of the university's first deaf president.

Within the deaf community, there are powerful cultural impediments to autobiographical and biographical narratives. The deaf community has continued to be somewhat segregated. Its cohesion and use of a different language, American Sign Language (ASL), has had the important value of forging community among deaf people, but this has complicated the process of reconnecting to mainstream hearing society. As with the languages of all oral cultures, ASL is unable to function as a written language. Thus, autobiography and biography of deaf lives must be written and published in the language of the majority hearing society.

Once written, the question arises as to how to classify these stories. Should deaf narratives be considered part of the new genre of disability studies? Do they belong in the category of minority group studies? The Deaf empowerment movement has been accompanied by the growing belief by many deaf and hearing people that the deaf community represents an oppressed linguistic and cultural minority. To many deaf people, deafness is not a medical condition that requires a cure. According to Couser, the obstacles to literary self-representation and representation of the deaf create a problem. Continued segregation will encourage the ongoing perception of deafness as a disability, rather than as a cultural/linguistic minority. However, all narratives of deaf lives offer a counterdiscourse that disables "stereotypes of disability" merely by the act of giving voice to deaf experiences.[16] The importance of these narratives lies in the portrayal of the life into which disability enters and intrudes, imposing marginality on the deaf person and how the deaf person deals with that state. For deaf people, the depiction of their own marginality similarly serves as an agent of their recovery in addition to being a means of self-expression.

In spite of the need to rethink the concept of life writing (including biography, autobiography, diary, and memoir) in its application to disability and deafness narratives, these genres that are "located on the borders of the literary"[17] are genres that are especially appropriate to individuals who are marginalized and, consequently, on the borders of society, according to Couser. Memoirs and autobiographies of deafness, in particular, seem to be entering a richer period. Each narrative offers a new view of the ways in which deafness can impact on life experience and interact with other factors, both physical and cultural: "Signing individuals have been given lasting and memorable traces on paper."[18]

These narratives of disability and deafness have value both for the storyteller and for the audience. The biographer may transmute painful experiences in art and may rise above adverse circumstances. Even if one cannot repair the situation and it ends badly, there is value in being able to describe and discuss it in literature. The fact that the tale can be told can reduce stigma and marginalization for the person recounting it.

These written narratives may provide help to other deaf and disabled people by giving them a different perspective on their situation, and friends of deaf people can support their friends more intelligently by reading such narratives and reflecting on them.

Particularly noteworthy is that through these narratives, deaf people can find meaning in their deafness. The writing serves as a healing ritual. According to Couser, "If illness and disability are reminders of our mortality and frailty, narratives of these conditions are testaments to our resilience and vitality."[19] Narratives at first take us out of our bodies and later return us to them with a better understanding of how bodies shape our identity. Illness or disability threaten to make our lives meaningless by fragmenting them. But by organizing our lives in coherent ways, these disability and deafness narratives shore up a sense of the value of these lives.

Disabled and deaf people, like women of previous centuries, had been made invisible. In part this situation was created by others: the society-at-large for deaf and disabled people and the male establishment for women. But the situation was complex, for the marginalized groups came to internalize and accept the diminished view of them propagated by mainstream culture, and they lost the belief that they could achieve heroic stature. Carolyn Heilbrun, in *Women's Lives: The View from the Threshold*, describes the courage it takes for those in a liminal or marginalized state to struggle against their isolation. Focusing in large measure on the situation of women, Heilbrun speaks of the realization on the part of early feminists that women had been made invisible as professionals, and how daring it was for these women to step outside of established societal structures and challenge the norm.

Heilbrun looks at the biographies and memoirs of women who struggled with a state of "betweenness." In so doing, they altered literature and society. How did such marginalization initially occur? Feminists believe that literature before and after World War I reflected what amounted to a war of the sexes. Professional women, particularly those who wrote, were consistently portrayed as evil and intruding upon men's clear right to be the only literary creators. Feminism came to see in modernism, the literature that prevailed during that era, a fear of women's voices that seemed to be its single most powerful motivation. Women are consistently seen in the works of this era as objects of men's desires or hatred; the women are not seen as capable of having a range of human experiences. And women who gave all their energy to writing, rather than trying to please men, were judged not to be worth looking at, either as women or as writers. Feminism, beginning in the 1960s, revealed this war of the sexes and, at the same time, in writing about it, revised the situation. Women in their writing and analyses began to portray a new range of possibilities.

The cost was high, however, for female writers dissenting from mainstream culture between World Wars I and II and even into more recent times. Such women were on the point of leaving one condition or self for another, but were not yet clear about where they belonged or what they should be doing. Heilbrun saw them as having a threshold experience, or being in a state of liminality. (The word *limen* means "threshold.") Women turned to liminality in order to find a way out of patriarchy. They needed to take stock, define a new direction, and find alternative communities to support them. The path was particularly challenging for women who wrote memoirs or biographies. When women memoirists write about being between worlds or experiences that are new, they must create a new form, as male autobiography doesn't provide them with adequate models. They discover themselves, become famous, and re-create themselves by the act of writing. Even if they don't conclude their works with the certainty of male autobiography, they do reflect a less apologetic tone than earlier female autobiography. These newer autobiographies have an admission of ambition and do not shy away from discussing the suffering the women experienced to attain their goals. Although these women had their individual goals and destinies, the desire for all of them was to move from this state of liminality, courageously chosen, to the center of human experience.

The female biographers portrayed in this study will be in a state of liminality in two arenas. They are caught between worlds both as deaf individuals and as women. Their somewhat ambivalent views of their deafness will be discussed at length in the chapters of the book devoted to them. Their views of themselves as women are equally complex, stemming in part from their belonging to two eras, as their education occurred in large measure during the late nineteenth century while their actual professional careers extended well into the twentieth century. Pitrois, although additionally challenged psychologically by a temporary blindness that had traumatized her in childhood, had great courage and energy in pursuing her writing career. Her works were well reviewed during her era, and she was decorated by several countries, including France and Belgium. She seemed to have had little conflict about pursuing her writing. This may have been due, to some extent, to the influence of her mother, who was well established as a writer of children's books in France and offered much encouragement to her talented daughter.

Corinne Rocheleau received more opposition from her family when she entered the work world, even though the decision to do so was, at least in part, due to financial considerations. It is true, though, that she took jobs in addition to her writing, working at the Census Bureau in Washington, D.C., and, later, at her brother's factory. This was still a more unusual path for a woman at that time than the teaching and writing that the family was more able to accept when she chose it as her full-time work later in her life. The differences between the responses of the families may also be culturally based. Pitrois traveled extensively, but her home and values were French. As a Franco-American who matured in both French Canada and the United States, Rocheleau and her family had values that belonged to the two cultures, but in this area, the family seemed to fall more into the American pattern of a reluctance to opening the work world to women. With impressive fortitude, Rocheleau followed her own path, eventually gaining the acceptance that she wanted, as she was close to her extended family.

Rocheleau challenged societal biases in other ways. For the women of her generation, the public and private spheres were separate. Women who wanted a public life did not marry, and for those who married, there was a private, but not a public, life. Already a well-known author,

Rocheleau married Wilfrid Rouleau later in life and had with him, according to her own accounting, her happiest years. He was very supportive of her achievements and was particularly proud of her writing success.

For those marginalized individuals in society—whether they are women or people who happen to be deaf, disabled, or ill—much courage is needed to tell their story. Negative portrayals in literature and the media and the absence of adequate role models still perpetuate stereotypes. And those writing to challenge these stereotypes encounter ridicule. But for those writing courageously in spite of such impediments, there is the possibility of self-discovery and re-creation of the self through the act of writing.

This was the path chosen by the three deaf writers included in this volume, which explores how they tell their stories of marginality, focusing in particular on how they crossed the divide between deaf and hearing people, each in his or her unique way. Although these biographers found different ways to bridge this gap, they are all brave, ethical, and civic-minded role models for us as readers, whether hearing or deaf. They teach us that it is possible, if challenging, to cultivate our uniqueness in a creative way while still participating in the larger society and making substantial contributions to it.

2 Crossing the Divide

*Yvonne Pitrois and Helen Keller Dialogue
about Disability*

How DOES the person living with a difference most effectively cross the cultural divide and explain herself to mainstream society? This is a central question raised by Yvonne Pitrois in her biography of Helen Keller entitled *Une nuit rayonnante: Helen Keller* (*A Shining Night: Helen Keller*), to which Helen Keller responded.

At the time that Pitrois's biography of Keller was published in 1922, Helen Keller (1880–1968) was known worldwide as an extraordinary deaf-blind American writer, activist, and socialist. She had already written and published *The Story of My Life* (1893); an autobiographical portrait of her early years, *The World I Live In* (1908), a world she described as shaped by sensations of touch; and *Out of the Dark* (1913), a book of socialist writings. Yvonne Pitrois (1880–1937), although relatively unknown today, was almost equally renowned in her country, France, and, in fact, throughout Europe during her lifetime for her social service and her biographical studies. By 1912 Pitrois had already launched her bimonthly magazine, *La Petite Silencieuse* (*The Little Silent Girl*), which provided articles and counseling for deaf women and short biographical sketches of unknown deaf heroes of her age. She had already written numerous longer biographical studies, including her biography of Lincoln, *Nobles Vies. Abraham Lincoln, le libérateur des esclaves* (1911) (*Noble Lives. Abraham Lincoln, the Liberator of the Slaves*) and her most famous work, her life of the first committed educator of deaf people in France, *La Vie de l'Abbé de l'Epée* (1912) (*The Life of the Abbé de l'Épée*). The two authors had gotten to know one another through the "Cosmopolitan

Correspondence Club," established in 1912 by Mrs. James Muir, a deaf woman from Australia. Her goal was to encourage deaf citizens worldwide, particularly artists and men and women of letters, to communicate with one another, form friendships, and support one another in their creative endeavors.

Pitrois was thus uniquely qualified to chronicle Helen Keller's life. As a fellow literary artist, she understood the particular challenges faced by the deaf writer. Any deaf writer may feel burdened by the need to create in isolation, by a sense of responsibility to serve as a role model for, and to sustain in other ways, those sharing her difference. She may feel a particular charge to create a life worthy of emulation by her brothers and sisters. The burden carried by the deaf writer, and the challenges of defining and exemplifying a creative and dignified life, are beautifully set forth in Pitrois's biography of Keller.

Pitrois was also a particularly good choice in that she herself had become both deaf and blind at the age of seven, probably as the result of sunstroke. Thus, Pitrois can, in some ways, be considered Helen Keller's French counterpart. Although Pitrois regained her sight, she remained

Portrait of Yvonne Pitrois. Courtesy of Michelle Balle of the Institut National de Jeunes Sourds.

deaf all her life. She never forgot those years without vision, however, and demonstrated throughout her career a passionate desire both to chronicle and to serve her deaf and deaf-blind contemporaries. Her biography of Helen Keller, in particular, reflects this empathy for the issues that disabled people need to address in their lives. She focuses, in particular, on the tension between self-definition and isolation and the need for the disabled person to connect in an appropriate way with the larger society.

This empathy that arises from Pitrois's own experience of disability is reinforced by her positive attitude toward challenge. Certainly Helen Keller's often stated belief that obstacles exist so that we can overcome them was shared by Pitrois. Both believed that we define ourselves and reconnect to others through education, hard work, and strength of will. Pitrois knew, however, that these values must be modeled for us all by an early teacher. Pitrois's mother, Marguerite Pitrois, an author in her own right, known for her books for children, had served that function for Yvonne. For this reason, perhaps, Pitrois was keenly aware of the equally dramatic impact that Anne Sullivan had had on the life of young Helen Keller, and Part 1 of the biography—by far the most powerful section of the book—recounts the story of Helen's rescue by her teacher, Anne Sullivan, after seven years of living in darkness and isolation, a prisoner of blindness and deafness. This section of the book is aptly entitled "La délivrance d'une âme" ("The Delivery of a Soul").

Helen had not been born deaf and blind, Pitrois tells us in her portrait. She was born into a wealthy family in Tuscumbia, Alabama, a beautiful and precocious child. She showed an early affinity for language, speaking her first words at the age of six months, to the delight of her doting parents. Before the age of two, however, she had been rendered incurably deaf and blind through an acute congestion of the brain and stomach, and from then on she was cut off from the world around her.

Her mother and father responded with despair to what Yvonne Pitrois called the "double night" of blindness and deafness. The child responded largely with frustration and anger. Unable to find the key to the world she inhabited, she clearly felt a profound sense of alienation: "When she noticed that her mother and her aunt were dressed differently, she understood that they were going to go out and showed by her gestures that she wanted to accompany them. Where were they going? What did they do on these walks, these visits? What did these strange encounters with other dark forms that she feverishly groped mean? As the years passed by . . . she sought, with increasing agony, to solve the indecipherable puzzle that life was for her."[1]

Later on, Keller would speak of her feelings of imprisonment in those early years: "It seemed to me that invisible hands held me prisoner and I made furious efforts to free myself. Finally, the need to communicate became so overpowering that hardly a day, hardly an hour passed without a new emotional outburst on my part."[2]

In her autobiography, *The Story of My Life*, Helen Keller describes this initial childhood rage as a reflection of her profound frustration and isolation. It is also well-depicted in William Gibson's *The Miracle Worker* (1959), a much-performed theatrical representation of the early part of the Helen Keller story. Led to Alexander Graham Bell by a family physician, the agonizing parents were told by him to contact the Perkins Institution in Boston. A deaf-blind girl named Laura Bridgman had already been successfully educated there, according to Bell. Perhaps, Bell thought, a teacher might be found for Helen as well, someone who was willing to travel to and live in Alabama.

Who was this predecessor of Helen Keller's? Born in 1829, Bridgman was well known by Americans in her day. She had lost her hearing and sight at the age of two, after becoming ill with scarlet fever. The then director of the Perkins Institution, Dr. Samuel Howe, undertook her education, teaching her to fingerspell, to read raised letters, and to write clearly. It was the first relatively successful education of a deaf-blind person in America and, arguably, in the world. Laura attained an impressive level of moral and intellectual development. She became a deeply religious person whose favorite quotation was: "God is Love."[3] Her entire life was spent living within the confines of the Perkins Institution. During her earlier years there, she was Howe's favorite student.

But the egocentric, imperious Howe increasingly lost interest in the fastidious, bright, but intense and demanding person Laura became as she matured. She died there, at the age of sixty, in 1889, to be forgotten by the press, by scholars, and by the larger public soon after her death. Fortunately, in the past few years, she has been rediscovered. Two biographies about her were recently published: Ernest Freeberg's *The Education of Laura Bridgman: First Deaf and Blind Person to Learn Language*, which emphasized the educational theories of Samuel Howe (2000) and Elisabeth Gitter's *The Imprisoned Guest: Samuel Howe and Laura Bridgman, the Original Deaf-Blind Girl*, a more empathetic study of the personality of Laura Bridgman (2001).

When the Kellers wrote to Michael Anagnos, director of the Perkins Institution, Bridgman was living her last few years of life there. After some sustained correspondence, Anagnos chose the young teacher Anne Sullivan for Helen. She was, at that time, a twenty-year-old who had herself been blind. Anne was not of Helen's social class. She had come to Perkins at fourteen as a charity case. She was the daughter of Irish immigrants who were illiterate and impoverished. Her mother died young of tuberculosis. Her father, an abusive alcoholic, abandoned her beloved younger brother and Anne, forcing them to seek refuge in the infamous state poorhouse at Tewksbury. Anne suffered the torment of seeing her younger brother die there. She had to remain there for four years, during which she was virtually blind and alone. She arrived at Perkins profoundly marked by these experiences. She was a survivor: brilliant, strong, and stubborn. These were qualities that would stand her in good stead at the Keller home. At first a student at Perkins Institution, after regaining her sight, Anne became a teacher there. Anne Sullivan had known Laura Bridgman (Anne had lived in the same cottage at Perkins as Laura in the 1880s, long before the request for help had come from the Kellers), and she had studied extensively the methods used with her and communicated with her in person before she left Massachusetts for Alabama.

In 1887 Anne Sullivan arrived at the Keller home and met her charge, a child whose behavior was wild and erratic. Through Anne's efforts

Helen gained language and a renewed connection to those around her. There were, at first, some notoriously unsuccessful efforts on the part of the teacher to reach her student, however, efforts to which Helen responded with unbridled anger. An infuriated Helen once locked Anne Sullivan in her room, and the latter needed to be rescued from it by Captain Keller, through a window, using a ladder. A special doll sent by the blind children at the Perkins Institution and dressed by Laura Bridgman herself was shattered by Helen in her frustration at being unable to understand the connection between Anne Sullivan's finger-spelling and the object spelled, as Anne tenaciously tried to convey to Helen the concept that every object has a name.

Finally, Anne led Helen to a well and pumped water onto one of Helen's hands, while fingerspelling "water" into the other. It became quickly apparent that the child had understood! The fact that this was one of a few words that Helen had retained from childhood had doubt-less helped Miss Sullivan to establish the necessary connection in young Helen's mind. After this linguistic awakening, Helen excitedly led Anne back into the house to "name" her mother, father, and sister. Thus, the chaos in the child's life receded, in favor of a life of meaning and order. Helen speaks in her autobiography of the profound transformation in her, once she could communicate with others. She no longer felt such intense rage, or had any desire to behave badly toward others.

Pitrois wisely sees that this first obstacle, the isolation through incomprehension, was the most challenging to deal with. But there were many steps that would have to follow this linguistic breakthrough. Helen had none of the basic skills of hearing and sighted children of her age. In three and a half months, however, under Miss Sullivan's tutelage, Helen learned to express herself, and to read and to write both in Braille and in ordinary script. Her intellectual development was rapid and impressive. She loved her studies and showed an early talent for writing that would continue to develop as she matured. Against all odds, she graduated from Radcliffe College in 1904, at the age of twenty-four, with a bachelor of arts degree and with honors in English.

Pitrois believed that these challenges posed by disability to Helen's intellectual development were well documented, not only by her, in her analysis, but by many other contemporary biographers. She felt, however, that the important challenges to ethical development that Helen faced had been less documented and were of equal importance. As Pitrois was a deeply religious French Protestant, she was particularly interested in offering evidence for, and an analysis of, Helen's evolution from an immoral, or at best amoral, child committing destructive acts to a deeply moral adult, who performed acts of charity and social service.

We see this transformation in the chapter entitled "La bonté d'Helen Keller" ("The Goodness of Helen Keller"). As early as the first Christmas in which she had language, Helen showed a profound generosity. She surrendered a new, treasured gift she had received, a goblet, to a poor child in Tuscumbia who had been standing near the Christmas tree in sadness because he had received no gifts at the party. This goodness of heart would only develop further as the child grew into adulthood. In her description of the mature Helen Keller who was her contemporary, Pitrois speaks of Helen's many contributions to society, including a massive correspondence with numerous friends and even strangers who needed her advice on issues related to disability.

It is only in the last four pages of the sixty-one-page manuscript that Pitrois had any ethical disagreements with, any real criticism of, her subject. A single choice on the part of Helen Keller tarnished her reputation for Pitrois and numerous other Europeans: it was her decision to allow herself to be drawn to the vaudeville stage and to perform with Anne Sullivan. For Pitrois, these theatrical performances were painful, offensive, and exhibitionistic.[4]

Did this display of theatricality have any redeeming value? Pitrois acknowledged that the performances may have helped people with disabilities. They may have shaken public indifference, awakening the crowds to the situation of deaf-blind people. They may have had some educational value for confused parents and educators, eager to help this population but unaware of the best ways to do this. Even those who came to the performances with the least noble motives, out of curiosity, Pitrois hoped, might have been inspired to examine and to improve their own lives and to admire the achievements of this woman.

While acknowledging that such transformations may have occurred, Pitrois cannot accept the means by which they were achieved. In the conclusion of her analysis, she still referred to these vaudeville performances as "fâcheuses excentricités" ("unfortunate eccentricities").[5] She couldn't see an application of Keller's writing to the vaudeville stage or Keller's assumption of the role of actor in this medium. For Pitrois, this was not an acceptable manner in which to cross the cultural divide between deaf and hearing people. She added, nonetheless, a positive note, trusting that the memory of these performances would be forgotten. What would be remembered, she hoped, about Helen Keller were the many fine traits and strengths she developed that turned her "double night" of blindness and deafness into a "shining night," the language chosen by Pitrois for the title of her study, because the words reflect the pure light of goodness that Pitrois saw emanating from Keller's personality.

Pitrois herself sent the completed copy of Helen Keller's biography to her subject and friend across the seas. Keller responded to the analysis in the biography, particularly the previously discussed criticism. Although it represented only a small part of the otherwise glowing portrait of her in Pitrois's work, she was distressed by the harsh words. She valued Pitrois's "sweet approval," for this friend in France had also led a silent life and knew the difficulties that deafness brought.[6]

Keller acknowledged the many similarities between their paths, as Pitrois had indicated, particularly the roles of their respective mentors. Because Pitrois had experienced "the wise ministrations of a gifted mother,"[7] she was able to understand how Anne Sullivan had similarly freed Helen Keller from the spiritual bondage and the isolation that often surrounded disabled people. Keller, consequently, recognized the appropriateness of having Pitrois as her biographer.

Keller took issue only with Pitrois's condemnation of her work in vaudeville. Her explanation for it and her defense of her choice are intriguing. Far from seeing herself as being drawn against her will into vaudeville and being exhibited on the stage like a wild animal, as Pitrois had implied, Keller explained that it was she who chose the lectures and work in vaudeville and persuaded Anne Sullivan to participate with her.

Why did she make this decision? Keller felt that she chose the vaudeville stage for several valid reasons. Reflecting the American spirit of enterprise, Keller expressed pride in being able to earn an independent living as an actor. She was also able to help her teacher financially. Although her teacher was highly praised, Keller explained, she had received little financial compensation for her work. Nor were she and Anne Sullivan the only disabled performers on the American vaudeville stage. Keller mentioned that she knew personally a deaf man who danced on the stage and two blind men who sang. Their performances were seen as manly attempts to earn their living; they were not seen as examples of the exploitation of disabled people by Americans, Helen Keller explained.

She refuted Pitrois's negative characterization of vaudeville as demonstrating an extreme instance of American commercialism and theatricality, with no redeeming features. Vaudeville, Keller believed, offered a means by which an actor, speaker, or artist could participate in society and do something worthwhile. Keller spoke often of the educational aspect of her vaudeville work. This was theatricality whose message, in her opinion, served a noble end. "Vaudeville is life in a nutshell,"[8] she wrote to Pitrois.

She, herself, Keller stated, had learned much about her country and countrymen as she traversed the United States from Maine to California. More profoundly, she believed that her experiences on the stage had helped her to understand human nature with its good and bad sides. But the dark or mean side, Helen Keller felt, came from ignorance and poverty. She did not feel that it came from evil.

Not only had she been enriched, Helen Keller continued, but others had benefited, as well. Her express goal was to cheer, through the message of her performance, deaf people, blind people, poor people, and soldiers who had been wounded in World War I, among others. She was motivated all her life by these humanitarian goals and felt that vaudeville offered her the opportunity to pursue them.

What was the nature of these performances that elicited such polarized responses from two exceptional women who, otherwise, appeared to have so much in common? Which of them had more correctly assessed these performances? The quest for answers led me back to the archives of the American Foundation for the Blind in New York City to consult their fairly extensive vaudeville file.

Among the materials was the copy of an actual script that Helen Keller and Anne Sullivan had used in their performance, written in dialogue form. The script told Keller's story, depicting her evolution from an isolated child who had only a few gestures with which to show what she wanted, to a world celebrity, the master, not only of English, but of French, German, and Italian.

Anne Sullivan performed a larger part of the dialogue. She spoke of her pupil's indomitable spirit in overcoming such formidable obstacles. Helen Keller had, at seven, when Sullivan first came to her, the vague memory of several spoken words and a few invented signs. Nodding her head meant "yes" and shaking it meant "no." Smacking her lips meant that she wanted candy. Recounting the story familiar to readers of *The Story of My Life*, Anne told of her struggles to teach Helen language, until she finally led her to the pump and Helen came to understand the word *water*. Sullivan also tells of Helen's hard work, successful to some extent, as she tried to learn to speak.

Following her teacher's introduction and discussion, Helen Keller appeared on the stage and, speaking for herself, concluded the twenty-minute act by offering a brief message of hope to humanity. Keller said that the gift of language from her teacher had helped her to find her soul, to find joy, and to find God. Her retrieval, she continued, proved that we all live by and for one another. God's most important commandment, said Keller, was "Love ye one another."[9] Keller moved from an appreciation of her teacher to praise of God as the curtain fell.

This act was followed by questions from members of the vaudeville audience. Some of the questions were trivial:

Question: How old are you?

To which Keller would quip, in answer, using one of the following formulas:

Answer: Between sixteen and sixty.

or

Answer: How old do I look?

or

Answer: There is no age in vaudeville.

But an equal number of questions were reflective and elicited responses in kind:

Question: What do you like best about your teacher?
Response: Her friendship.
Question: What have you enjoyed doing most in life?
Answer: Overcoming difficulties.
Question: What virtue do you admire most?
Answer: Intellectual honesty.
Question: What is the ideal result of education?
Answer: A thinking mind and an understanding heart.[10]

An analysis of the act itself and a majority of the questions and answers would seem to give validity to Keller's assertion in a letter to her friend Daisy Sharpe that, "We had a dignified little act."[11] In that same letter, however, she acknowledged to Daisy that at first she had found it alien to be on the vaudeville stage with trained animals, dancers, and acrobats. Thus Helen, like this reader, agreed that certain aspects of the work in vaudeville were, indeed, somewhat crass and commercial. Nonetheless, she chose to remain in vaudeville between 1920 and 1924.

Why did she do so? Helen Keller fully accepted the American view and saw vaudeville as an acceptable, even a desirable, form of theater. Many actors who continued their careers on the legitimate stage had their beginnings in this unique theatrical form. And Helen had a particular fascination with actors and the theater. In 1918, a few years prior to the vaudeville experience, Keller had been invited to go to Hollywood to film her life story. The idea for the film had come from a popular historian named Frances Trevelyan Miller.[12] Keller, herself, had come up with the title for the film, "Deliverance." The film was well reviewed but did not succeed at the box office. Keller, however, had delighted in the opportunity to perform in a blond wig and white make-up and, above all, to meet stars like Mary Pickford, Douglas Fairbanks, and Charlie Chaplin, who was one of her heroes.

When the opportunity to perform in vaudeville presented itself, Keller didn't hesitate. Always an extrovert, she loved the adventure of vaudeville and the people that it brought into her life. "I found the world of vaudeville much more amusing than the world I had always lived in, and I liked it. I liked to feel the warm tide of human life pulsing round and round me. . . . I enjoyed watching the actors in the workshop of faces and costumes."[13] Feeling independent as a performer on the stage, guided by the scent of roses placed on the stage daily for that purpose, and taught to do her own makeup by the famous singer-performer Sophie Tucker, Keller flourished on the vaudeville stage. And vaudeville enjoyed Helen Keller, as well. She developed into a great success for them, became a so-called headliner who always played to capacity crowds and was well regarded by the spectators.[14] Consequently, Keller easily chose it over other possible ways of earning her living with Anne Sullivan: the rigors of a lecture tour circuit, which necessitated rapid travel to many places in succession and the pressures and less social activity of writing.

Why did Yvonne Pitrois's feelings about vaudeville differ so dramatically from those of her friend and colleague? Of a more retiring nature than Helen Keller, Pitrois found this medium very alien. Her timidity is discussed in an article by E. Drouot, a critic who was her contemporary.[15] Was this shyness the result of the childhood trauma, the sudden loss of hearing and temporary loss of sight that she experienced at seven? It is reasonable to assume that that was a significant contributing factor. The state of medical care in 1887 could not offer much in the way of treatment for this doubly disabling condition. Doctors could only urge Marguerite Pitrois, Yvonne's mother, to keep her daughter in a quiet dark room; they prescribed rest. Taught and consoled by her mother, Yvonne Pitrois struggled between light and darkness, regaining her vision fairly completely at about the age of twelve but remaining deaf for the rest of her life. Pitrois seemed accepting of her deafness, but in spite of the recovery of her sight, she was profoundly affected by the temporary experience of its loss, and her biographies reflect that preoccupation. Images suggesting a tension between light and darkness abound in her texts. Even the titles of her works reflect this obsession: *Ombres de Femmes* (*Shadows of Women*), *Une nuit rayonnante: Helen Keller* (*A Shining Night: Helen Keller*), and *Trois lumières dans la nuit: Valentin Haüy, Louis Braille, Maurice de la Sizeranne* (*Three lights in the Darkness . . .*), among others.

Aware of this vulnerability, Pitrois's mother, to help her overcome this timidity and retain the speech that she was in danger of losing, sent her out to various merchants to perform the errands of the household. The strategy was successful in helping her to learn to lipread others and to make herself understood. It also helped Pitrois not to become paralyzed by her shyness. In time, she developed the initiative to pursue a professional career as a writer, publishing her first work at the age of eighteen. Her personality, however, was always less expansive than that of Helen Keller. She was a private person, whose many acts of kindness were done with little fanfare. Thus, it is easy to understand why the concept and experience of vaudeville were very foreign to her psychologically.

As Pitrois wrote very little about herself directly, we need to analyze her biographies of others to uncover the cultural and societal events and attitudes that may have shaped her opinions. She had a lifelong concern about the misunderstanding and mockery to which disabled people had been subjected and continued to be subjected in Europe. In *La Vie de l'Abbé de l'Épée* (*The Life of the Abbé de l'Épée*), Pitrois portrayed, emotionally and at great length, the societal bias and myths about deaf people that tormented the mother of the deaf twins in this work. The mother here is clearly a "porte-parole" or stand-in for Pitrois herself.

What exactly might she have feared from a vaudeville performance? In a later work, Pitrois sketches her nightmare scenario. Valentin Haüy, one of the three heroes featured in *Trois lumières dans la nuit . . .*, was a sighted man who devoted his career to the cause of the blind. Pitrois portrays, in this sketch, the moment he decided to do so.

In 1771, at the age of twenty-six, walking through the streets of Paris, Haüy saw ten blind men grotesquely dressed in long robes, with pointed hats and fake eyeglasses, seated on a makeshift stage. They were being exhibited at a street fair, and the crowd was laughing at them and ridiculing them. The organizers of the fair, in a final insulting touch, had the blind men playing violins, although they had no musical training. Haüy was horrified by the spectacle. He determined to make it possible for the blind to learn to read and, eventually, to earn a living in a dignified way. True to his vow, he developed a system of raised letters, a precursor of Braille, and spent most of his life teaching blind children, a life not without other challenges.

Pitrois is clearly distressed in the retelling of this story. She personally intervenes in her narrative on page 3 of her study of Valentin Haüy, included in *Trois lumières dans la nuit*, to express her horror at those who display the blind men for profit and at the cruelty of the audience laughing at them. Sharing the view of her hero, Haüy, Pitrois has the moral conviction that blind people have the right to education and a dignified life. I believe that she saw theatrical spectacle, in general, as having the potential of going awry for a disabled person. No wonder, then, that she disagreed vehemently with the notion that vaudeville could be a means of positive expression and activity for a deaf-blind person. Pitrois wanted respect and dignity for deaf and deaf-blind people, as did Helen Keller. But unlike Helen Keller, she did not see exhibitionism and spectacle as the path that led to this respect.

Although the two women differed in the way each chose to bridge the social divide, they were equally impressive in their brilliance, in their passion for language and writing, and in their wish to serve others limited by disability. They shared a desire to encourage disabled people to transcend the solitary life for a richer one. Ably educated and encouraged to overcome their limitations by their respective mentors, they became accomplished human beings. As the achievements of both were considerable, and although their positions in some areas were diametrically opposed, they illustrate the importance of not depicting a single mode of self-realization as the correct one for any deaf or deaf-blind person.

Further, they provide admirable examples as to how to conduct a dialogue and deal with diversity (for we have a diversity in perspective here) in a creative and an intelligent way. Although they strongly disagreed, they remained colleagues who collaborated. In the very letter in which she dialogued with Pitrois, Helen Keller enclosed an article for her. It was an article that Pitrois had requested for her periodical, *La Petite Silencieuse* (*The Little Silent Girl*). She enclosed it, Helen Keller states, in the hope that it would comfort some deaf-blind readers. "Will you accept it," she writes, "with my love and warm comradeship in a never ceasing fight against cruel limitations?"[16]

This commonality of purpose bound the two more than any difference in strategy for explaining oneself to the world could divide them. And in their acceptance of one another's divergent views, they teach us, almost a century later, the power of tolerance and the importance of openness to different perspectives.

3 Jean-Ferdinand Berthier

The Development of an Activist

Jean-Ferdinand Berthier (1803–1886) was a deaf militant before the age of militants, an ardent defender of sign language and a promoter of the emancipation of deaf people. He was, as well, a skilled writer of treatises, essays, and biographies. His life was spent in an effort to encourage deaf people to celebrate sign language, while at the same time inviting hearing people to share in this rich heritage. The desire to break down the barriers between the deaf and the hearing worlds was a constant in his life, although his thinking altered as to the best way to bridge the gap.

In spite of his many talents and the seriousness of his concerns, however, Berthier's life and work were forgotten by the larger public until recently.[1] To understand this, we have to look at events in the age in which Berthier lived, particularly the role of the Congress of Milan in 1880. The focus of this international meeting was on eradicating the use of sign language in schools and classes for deaf children. Although the Congress did not have legal authority, it passed resolutions that had a profound impact on deaf people for most of the next century.[2]

The largest number of attendees came from Italy (157) and from France (67). (One deaf person, alone, was there, out of sixty-seven French Congress attendees, Claudius Forestier, a friend of Berthier's, director of the Deaf Institute in Lyon.) Other countries had a very small representation. England had twelve delegates; Germany had eight; America had six, and there was one delegate from each of the

Jean-Ferdinand Berthier. Courtesy of Armand Pelletier and Yves Delaporte of the CLSFB.

following countries: Belgium, Canada, Russia, Norway, and Sweden.*
The Congress declared the superiority of speech over signs in returning
deaf people to society and in giving them a more perfect knowledge of

---

*There is some controversy over the number of attendees as well as over the number
of attendees who were actual voting members of the Congress of Milan. But many

language. The delegates overwhelmingly endorsed the use of the oral method in the instruction of deaf children. In effect, the resolution eliminated the use of sign language in all educational settings, leaving it to exist only in the community of deaf adults.

The results of the Congress can be seen to have been politically orchestrated by the French and Italian delegates. France, after 1870, sought national and linguistic unity and did not want to support a deaf minority culture and language. Further, there was a desire for the establishment of smaller private schools for the deaf on the part of the bourgeoisie. They wanted smaller schools because they didn't like the mixture of social classes in the larger institutions and thought their children would benefit more from smaller schools that would permit them to be day pupils. As these were created quickly to supplant the national institutions, there was no time to teach the instructors sign language. Oralism became the only viable alternative.[3]

The destructive effects of the rulings of the Milan Congress soon became evident. Deaf teachers all but disappeared from schools for the deaf. Instead of being better integrated into society, deaf people communicated less well with both hearing and deaf people. This led them to choose professions like gardening, carpentry, and shoemaking that could be done in relative isolation, while more intellectual and social opportunities for those so inclined were lost. It was not until thirty years later, in 1910, that there was a softening of the position on oralism in France. At the Institut National de Jeunes Sourds (National Institute for Deaf Children), where Berthier had spent his professional career, students were finally allowed to use sign outside of class again and a pedagogy developed that was based more on written language than on

---

French historians, including Christian Cuxac, wrote that 157 or 158 attendees came from Italy, and 67 came from France.

Of these attendees, however, only between 164 and 167 delegates could vote. Fifty-six of these official delegates were French oralists, and 66 were Italian oralists. Together, the oralists from France and Italy represented 74 percent of the Congress. It was clear that the Congress was planned by a committee that sought to ensure the defeat of sign language.

The Institut National de Jeunes Sourds in Paris in 1894 (Berthier died in 1886).

speech. The negative effects of the Congress were acknowledged and finally acted on and reversed, at least to some extent.

Berthier, however, did not live to see these positive changes. His life came to an end in Paris on July 12, 1886, only six years after the Congress of Milan. He died, at the age of eighty-three, at his home on Boulevard Saint-Germain, and he was buried in Sagy. His life had been challenging. In spite of his convictions about the value of sign language, he had watched, particularly during the latter part of his career, the spreading influence of oralism and the negative image of the deaf child that was projected by those who should have validated him or her.

Berthier had seen and helped to create excellent moments in the development of the French deaf community, but he must also have learned of Milan's ruling to use speech to teach deaf people and to abolish the use of sign language. Although Berthier did not write about his reaction to the Congress directly, his friend Claudius Forestier, who was the director of the institute for the deaf in Lyon, refuted the conclusions of the Milan Congress in "Parallèle entre l'instruction des sourds-muets par le langage des signes et leur enseignement par l'articulation artificielle" (Lyon: Imprimerie Pitrat aîné, 1883) ("Comparison between the Instruction of the Deaf through Sign Language and Their Instruction through Speech"). The language used in this essay, the particular arguments made, were the same that Berthier himself had employed to reject oralism throughout his career. Without doubt, he must have known of the resolutions and Forestier's response to them, and it must have been a bitter moment for him.

No man's life can or should be measured only by his last years, and Berthier's is no exception. In his lifetime, he acquired a reputation for the breadth of his knowledge, for his deep devotion to the cause of deaf people and for his many successes in fighting for deaf rights. He was so revered by the deaf community of his era that he became known as "the creator of the silent nation" and "the Napoleon of the deaf."[4] In an effort to highlight these positive contributions, in the climate of an awakening of deaf culture in the past few decades, the Ferdinand Berthier Cultural and Sign Language Society was founded by Armand Pelletier and Yves Delaporte. Its goal was to celebrate Berthier's heritage in France, to publish works by and about him, and to organize events that would commemorate Berthier's life and contributions.

Berthier was born on October 1, 1803, in Louhans of an old family from Sagy. Although he himself said he was born deaf, perhaps trying to create a personal myth or wanting to eliminate any distance between himself and the deaf community, most critics believe that he became deaf at four, as the result of a childhood illness. A brother who was a doctor and other specialists of the era were unable to cure him, so it was decided to send him to the Royal Institution for the Deaf (later renamed the National Institute for the Deaf and referred to as such hereafter) in Paris on Saint-Jacques Street in 1811. The Abbé Sicard had been its director since 1794. The earliest years of Berthier's youth and schooling there pointed to his great gifts. He had, as well, excellent instructors at the National Institute who aided in his development. Among them were Bébian, Pelletier, and Paulmier. He had a profound attachment to the school.

By 1813 Berthier was seriously interested in drawing and had become one of the finest art students at the National Institute. Sicard had decided to introduce his two best students to Louis XVIII. Berthier had been one of them. He offered a portrait he had made of Henry IV, drawn in pencil, to King Louis XVIII, which the king was happy to accept from Berthier, whose talents were impressive. It was assumed that Berthier would choose to earn his living as an artist. With his classes finished, Berthier left to live with his brother on rue Dauphine, at the home of their uncle. Berthier's artistic gifts earned him a position working for an engraver.

An analysis of one of his key drawings, "L'homme au serpent" ("The Man with a Snake"), gives us some insight into the young Berthier's psyche and concerns. This was a symbolic drawing done by Berthier when he was twenty. In this drawing, a serpent seems to be coming out of the man's mouth. How can one interpret this odd composition?

Drawing by Berthier, "L'homme au serpent." Courtesy of Armand Pelletier and Yves Delaporte of the CLSFB.

What does the snake stand for? Why is it emerging from the man's mouth? In Christian thought, the serpent is evil. In the garden of Eden, it was the serpent who incited Adam and Eve to sin. This imagery was well known to deaf students at the school founded by the Abbé de l'Épée and later directed by the Abbé Sicard. The emergence of the snake from the man's mouth illustrated a recurrent theme in the Bible, that what comes out of man's mouth is bad.

Among the impure things that come out of the mouth is speech; the Bible often mentions it as such. It can be dangerous to speak, and certainly, silence is superior to speech. It has a mystical dimension; it is the only means of reaching God and is often accompanied by ascetic practices that lead to self-mastery. As early as the sixth century, the monks observed a rule of silence, and this practice of silence led to the development of a sign language that the monks would henceforth use. In this drawing by the twenty-year-old Berthier, we already see Berthier's preoccupation with the division between deaf and hearing people and his belief in the beauty and power of sign language. He had little appetite for vocal speech and communicated with the hearing only by writing to them. His favored means of communication was his beloved sign language.[5] Art became for Berthier, even this early, a means of expressing his views and mediating them, a phenomenon that similarly occurred in his later biographical writings.

Berthier decided that he wanted a future as a teacher, rather than as an artist, and with the support of his former teacher and friend, Auguste Bébian, he secured a post at the Paris institute. He was named provisional assistant-master in 1820. A small disappointment early on in Berthier's career seemed to foreshadow the many he would experience at the Deaf Institute in Paris. In 1824, the duke of Berry visited the institute and chatted with Berthier at length. He was so charmed by Berthier's talent that he promised him an allowance of three hundred francs. In spite of follow-up letters in 1825 and 1826, Berthier never received this sum from the duke. This was one small betrayal on the part of a hearing person. Unfortunately, there would be many others.

Soon after Berthier's arrival, the institute was in transition. Bébian was forced to leave in 1821, and the Abbé Sicard died in 1822. These events left the institute in a state of chaos. In the classes, there was no cohesion in method or in sign languages. Some instructors had remained faithful to the methodical signs of the Abbé de l'Épée, while others adhered to the theories of Sicard, developed in 1808. Sicard's method was based on the observation of the mime of deaf children. Still other teachers followed their own inclinations. This left a vacuum, which was filled by Désiré Ordinaire, a doctor who became the new director of the Paris institute in 1831. In the late 1820s and early 1830s, four circulars were sent through the institute that foreshadowed the ascent of oralism. Under Ordinaire's leadership, oralism began to take hold. Regardless of their level of deafness, all children had to speak; signs were prohibited. The attacks against sign language became more numerous and more specific. The three major deaf instructors at the Paris Institute, Berthier, Lenoir, and Forestier, were demoted, and a "rotation system" was established, replacing the "transmission system."

Until 1830, each teacher at the National Institute was responsible for a class at a given level. When the students were ready to transfer into a higher class, they were given a new teacher. Each year, the teachers would transfer their students to another teacher. This procedure was called the "transfer" or "transmission system." By 1832 a new system had been established—the "rotation system." Under this system, teachers would stay with the same students for six years, or throughout their schooling. Since deaf teachers were unable to teach the oral training classes, they were excluded from all principal teaching duties and had to accept inferior tasks at inferior pay. Most were demoted to the role of tutors or assistants to the hearing teachers. In effect, they lost all status at the institute.

Berthier fought mightily against this new rotation system. He wrote three letters to Désiré Ordinaire and four letters to the board of directors. In reply, he received only two brief responses from Désiré Ordinaire; yet Berthier's critique was intelligent and moving.

He pointed out to the board that all teachers, beginners and advanced, would have the same students. Surely it was better to have the

most experienced teachers teach the most advanced students. He pointed to the injustice of the system's establishment. In a vote that had been
held among the faculty, four teachers out of six had voted against it, but
the rotation system was established anyway. The new system was harm-
ful to the students, too, in allowing for the use of several different teaching methods, instead of a single, rigorous approach to teaching. Under
the rotation system, each teacher had his own manner of instructing,
which the individual could modify without external control.

By far his most moving comments to the board were in his letter of
September 17, 1832. He signaled a humiliating distinction that had been
made between the hearing and the deaf teachers, to the detriment of
the deaf teachers. He spoke of his long service, his earned title, the difficulties that he had had to overcome in order to perform his duties. He
would have thought, he said, that such credentials made him at least
the equal of his hearing colleagues. He appealed to the spirit of justice
of the directors and to their presumed concern for the deaf: "Vous êtes
les protecteurs des sourds-muets, vous êtes leurs pères adoptifs" ("You
are the protectors of the deaf, you are their adoptive fathers"). Once
again, the theme of extreme disappointment in these hearing guardians
of the deaf students surfaces.[6]

A major issue in one of Berthier's letters to Désiré Ordinaire was his
concern that the value of sign language was being dismissed and
ignored. He defended the power, rapidity, and clarity of his beloved
language. He took on the thorny question of the clear superiority of
the deaf teachers in using this medium and discussed the inability of
hearing teachers to communicate well with their students.

Berthier spoke of his belief that he was the representative of his deaf
brothers in this same letter. For twelve years, he stated, he saw it as his
task to work for the moral regeneration of deaf people. His hope was to
prove that a deaf person was not less than a hearing person. But, Berthier stated, in the very heart of his own institution, the recent decree
destroyed his dream because it made the deaf an inferior class again:
"comme un genre mitoyen entre l'homme et la bête" ("like a species
midway between man and the animal").[7]

Ironically, the rotation system was bypassed to some extent, and Berthier was given the poorest students, taken from other classes. This was most probably punishment for his opposition to the administrative initiatives of Ordinaire and the board. Even with such students, however, Berthier proved himself a thoughtful, dedicated teacher. In a communication with Désiré Ordinaire, he explained many of the ideas that guided him professionally.

He wanted deaf children to be able to understand the world, for they would soon be thrown into it without anyone to guide them in their daily lives. He regretted that there was not enough time allotted in class for the students to be taught their rights and duties as citizens. His program of studies for 1834–1835, sent to Ordinaire at his request, was a rigorous one, given the level of the students. Some of his approaches were very creative. He told stories in sign language to his students, who had to translate them into written French. They studied grammatical rules, vocabulary, written French, and knowledge of the world. Even the weakest of Berthier's students, Dermigny, who was notorious in the National Deaf Institute for his failure to learn almost anything in the course of his years there, still had his own individual program of study, personally created by Berthier. In the course of the year, Dermigny learned complete conjugations of regular and irregular verbs, simple prepositions, and possessive pronouns and he was able to write short sentences from a signed dictation.

Berthier graded and grouped his students according to their abilities. He took notes on their character, conduct, and work. He wrote extensively about the eight poor students he had during the 1834–1835 school year. In spite of the regrettable level of Berthier's students, four of the eight miraculously made progress, attesting to the excellence of Berthier's teaching methods. Even a hostile administration could not find fault with these results.

When, in 1835–1836, Berthier was again given the weakest students, now twelve of them instead of eight, he protested strongly to the administration as he sent in his report on the students' progress, revealing a justifiable bitterness, possibly thinking, in particular, of his struggles to teach the unteachable Dermigny: "Voilà, Monsieur le Directeur, ce que j'ai pu faire avec des élèves mal assortis, de divers âges et de divers degrés de capacité, que les autres ont appelé des ânes peut-être avec raison" ("There you have, Mr. Director, what I was able to do with a poorly assorted group of students, of varied ages and abilities, that others have, perhaps correctly, labeled donkeys").[8] But even in such trying circumstances, Berthier softened his criticism of the students by saying that even such students could make progress, but only with great effort on the part of the instructor. He tried to make the point that twelve such students would be an unfair burden to any teacher. Ordinaire, however, remained unresponsive to Berthier's comments.

Berthier often spoke of his rights and those of the deaf teachers in general. Ordinaire's concern for the institute, he felt, should extend to the deaf professors who had a unique relationship with the institution. In a written communication with Ordinaire, he traced his own special connection to the Paris institute. The institute had raised him from the cradle and he had been brought up by the institute's teachers. Berthier appreciated this as a gift and tried to respond to it by offering help to his companions. His desire was to develop his skills sufficiently so that he could, one day, find ways to support the development of his deaf brothers. How then could Ordinaire not similarly care for his deaf teachers? Should an institution not take better care of its own?

Most of these questions remain unanswered. Berthier's positions did not reflect his true potential. He had numerous talents and was worthy of all the posts he had aspired to in addition to his role as teacher. He had applied for, and been denied, positions as librarian archivist, assistant director, and general inspector of studies. His qualifications were ignored, while others with less talent got ahead of him; only his deafness was considered, and it was seen only as a detriment. Through the ignorance of those making the appointments, deafness was not seen as an advantage for those teaching deaf children, and Berthier's understanding of the needs of deaf students was ignored.

Berthier came to feel, correctly, that deaf people lacked professional opportunities. Additionally, those who were able to work as professionals received poor remuneration compared to their hearing colleagues. Although the issue for Berthier was more about the need for dignity, rather than money, he, often with the support of his deaf colleague Lenoir, protested to the administration on the issue of salaries. But an adjustment was only made five years before Berthier's retirement. Once again, Berthier felt a mixture of sadness and bitterness.

In spite of conflicts on the job, Berthier was eminently well qualified as a teacher. He came from a distinguished family that valued education and professionalism. Among the noteworthy members of his family were a grandfather who was a notary, a father who was a surgeon, and an older brother who was a doctor. The family, consequently, had social and political weight in the region, which Berthier sometimes tried to use to his advantage.

Berthier's intelligence and desire to excel were valued early on by his teachers and colleagues. Paulmier, who had been one of young Berthier's teachers, spoke of his enormous intelligence. He told the story of Berthier coming to talk with him as a young student and asking how he could develop his intelligence. He explained that he wanted to be a genius like Clerc.[9] His students similarly admired him, speaking of his penchant for order, his love of learning, and his desire to inculcate the same in his students. He was kind but demanding, and his students both loved and respected him.

From his first to his last acts, he showed a desire for fairness, along with a humility and a sense of gratitude toward those who were a part of his life. We see all of these traits reflected in the will that he wrote in 1875, when he was seventy-two.[10] Having neither wife nor children, he shared his earthly goods and personal objects equitably among his loved ones, friends, and organizations in which he believed.*

He gave more to his nieces, Élise Pariset, Olympe Gelot, and Constance Lagrange, because their financial situation was more precarious than that of his nephews, who had received legacies from a grandmoth-

---

* He didn't forget the region of his birth and left an important sum to the major hospital of Louhans and the poor of Sagy.

er and from Berthier's brother. This is clearly explained in the will so that no one would feel hurt or unjustly treated after Berthier's death.

He entrusted himself to God's mercy and forgiveness and, in a spirit of humility, asked pardon for his errors and sins. Finally, he offered a beautiful thank-you to the friends and family closest to him and expressed his gratitude for the charm with which they graced his days. All of these character traits: his love for what was right, his reflective spirituality, and his ability to feel gratitude were among the traits that teachers, colleagues, and students admired in Berthier.

But the times and the situation demanded aggression and activism if the situation of deaf people was to be improved. And so, for the greater part of his life, we see a more militant side of his personality come forth in his roles as teacher, writer, and representative of the deaf community.

By 1838 Ordinaire had left the institute, and the political situation at the school finally improved. The deaf teachers, including Berthier, were reintegrated in terms of function and salary. But Berthier had seen clearly the vulnerable situation of deaf people and the deep divide that existed between hearing and deaf people on many educational and social issues. And during this difficult time, he discovered his strength and calling as a deaf activist and committed himself to a role beyond that of teacher.

Berthier's life increasingly reflected his engagement in the struggle to protect the rights of his deaf brothers and sisters. He worked to commemorate deaf history, promoting the building of the tomb of the Abbé de l'Épée at Saint-Roch and of his statue at Versailles. He sent letters to Parliament concerning the laws that governed the lives of deaf people in France, for he wanted to improve their social status. His goal was to have the law recognize the rights of deaf people as equal to those of the hearing. He was courageous in protesting to government officials and newspapers when this was not the case.

When he was prevented from serving as a witness at a friend's wedding, he persisted. The mayor had said that Berthier's use of sign language, rather than speech, might invalidate the marriage, believing that to be a witness, a person had to be able to hear and pronounce. Berthier knew that the mayor was in error and that such a law, if it existed, made no sense. Berthier saw in the mayor's position a reinforcement of the belief that sign language did not proceed from human intelligence in the same way that the spoken word did. Fortunately, when the wedding party arrived at Saint-Sulpice church, the clergy admitted the deaf husband as well as the deaf witness (Berthier) with no challenge, and the ceremony took place. And Berthier commented that "Dieu ouvre ses bras à tous les hommes, qu'ils parlent ou qu'ils ne parlent pas, parce que tous sont ses enfants" ("God opens his arms to all men whether or not they speak, because they are all his children").[11]

The exclusion of deaf people made Berthier aware of their vulnerable position in society and led him to continue to mobilize his talents on their behalf. The banquets he organized for deaf people were in response to this denigration. He organized the first banquet celebrating the birth of the Abbé de l'Épée, which was held on November 30, 1834, at the "Veau qui tête" restaurant on Chatelet Square. Some fifty-two guests attended this banquet, whose goal was to reinforce deaf solidarity and deaf creativity. Bernard Mottez, one of the leading chroniclers of the banquets, sees this as the date of the birth of the deaf nation.[12] It was decided that these banquets would be held annually.

Who participated in these banquets? An elite of the deaf community came. The men represented a variety of professions: professors, engravers, painters, printers, workmen, but they all were educated. International deaf men who were in Paris for a stay came to the banquets. By the third banquet, there were guests from Italy, Germany, and England. No women attended the banquets until 1883. In this regard the deaf community mirrored hearing society, for in the early nineteenth century, the place of women was still in the home.

Over time hearing people were also invited. At the first such banquet, only two hearing men attended: Eugène de Monglave (whose sign was "mustache"), who signed well and was viewed as a friend of the deaf, and M.B. Maurice, who was editor of a daily newspaper, *Le temps*. Maurice was the only person unable to communicate at the banquet, as he did not know sign language. In time, more hearing men were invited. Men in the government, journalists and, once the oralist approach ended at the deaf institute in Paris, the director, the personnel and even some students from the school were asked to attend. These banquets had multiple goals. They honored the memory of the Abbé de l'Épée and offered the deaf elite the opportunity to enjoy one another's company. But they also served to weave a network of relationships with hearing people who had influence in the press, in the administration, and in politics.

In spite of the opening of the banquets to the hearing, accusations persisted that deaf people wanted to enclose themselves in a ghetto. Berthier offered as a countercharge that hearing people had always wanted to exclude the people and steal sign language from them. Instead, said Berthier, let hearing people come to the banquets and experience and share deaf culture. He invited hearing people to learn sign and to reach out to the deaf community, bound by the links of language and culture.[13]

At the banquets, there was a celebration of French Sign Language (LSF). Its grace, dignity, and elegance were displayed by excellent signers like Berthier, Forestier, and Lenoir. Similarly, there was a celebration of the Abbé de l'Épée. Toasts were made to this spiritual father of deaf people, who was seen as having brought them from a state of exile into community. The banquets were also an opportunity for political activity. In the minutes of the banquets, the dreams, projects, struggles, and failures of deaf people are very apparent. The disagreements were there, as well, similar to today's dissensions and conflicts. In 1843 Berthier was named president for life of the banquets, to honor his commitment to helping deaf people find a place in society.

He had encouraged the members of the deaf community to think of themselves as a nation, and he became the first worthy leader of that nation. To serve his deaf brothers, he founded the Universal Society of the Deaf in the spring of 1838. Its goals were to promote friendly relationships among deaf people and to enlighten them as to their rights and duties.

Desiring to broaden the scope of his activities still further, Berthier presented himself as a candidate for the Constituent Assembly. He wanted to represent the two hundred deaf in Paris. He saw no reason for excluding deaf people from the assembly and indicated that he would be able to serve by relying on written texts and having others read aloud his speeches. By representing the Parisian deaf community, Berthier believed he could benefit all twenty-two thousand French deaf people. Although he was not elected, he had made an important political statement on behalf of the deaf community.

Perhaps the most significant honor that Berthier received was the award of the cross of the Legion of Honor. Berthier was only forty-six when Louis-Napoléon Bonaparte named him a recipient in August of 1849, at the time of the latter's first visit to the deaf institute in Paris. Berthier's honor was greatly respected by the deaf community then and now, and a name sign was recently developed for Berthier by the Berthier Association and indicated "the one who received the Legion of Honor."[14]

Berthier inspired and encouraged the artistic spirit that developed among the deaf people of his era. An evolution could be seen in all art forms: sculpture, painting, engraving, lithography, and poetry and literature. Art increasingly reflected the aspirations of this minority. The mobilization of deaf artists was accompanied by enlisting hearing artists to support their deaf counterparts. A noteworthy example was Parfait Merlieux, a hearing sculptor who was commissioned by the Central Society of the Deaf to create a bust of the Abbé de l'Épée. It is currently at the National Institute for the Deaf in Paris, but it was inaugurated in 1836, at the annual banquet of the deaf.

ALTHOUGH BEST known as an activist and champion of deaf causes, Berthier's life reflected his desire to break down the walls between hearing and deaf people, a desire that skirmishes with Désiré Ordinaire and the imperfect laws in France of that era could not destroy. He showed sadness and anger at the reverses but seemed to remain hopeful that such a rapprochement could occur. The banquets he organized, as well as other organizations and activities that he sponsored for the deaf community, demonstrated that hope.

In the face of so few good relationships with hearing people, how did he find and learn from models of tolerance and connection? It is largely in his writings that Berthier reveals the pitfalls in, and ultimately the triumphs of, complicated cross-cultural relationships. Though Berthier is better known as an activist than as a biographer, writing enabled him to transcend his disillusionments. He chronicled the lives of the intellectual elite at the Paris school of his era in biographical studies of Bébian, the Abbé de l'Épée, and the Abbé Sicard.

❦

AUGUSTE BÉBIAN was a natural choice as a biographical subject for Berthier. In 1813 Bébian was Berthier's teacher. The two were very fond of one another from their earliest days together. Berthier particularly admired Bébian's belief and proficiency in an authentic sign language. He had a grasp of sign language that was unusual for a hearing person. Bébian came to his profession through his relationship with Sicard. He was Sicard's godson, and the abbé introduced him to the work and served as his mentor. But Bébian went well beyond the methodological principles of his godfather. He believed that bilingualism was the best means of teaching deaf children, and he wanted sign language and French to be used together.

Bébian became an impressive scholar and author. His major works included *Essai sur les sourds-muets et sur le langage naturel, ou Introduction à une classification naturelle des idées avec leurs signes propres* (1817) (*Essay on the Deaf and on the Natural Language, or Introduction to a Natural Classification of Ideas with Their Appropriate Signs*); and *Mimographie ou essai d'écriture mimique, propre à régulariser le langage des sourds-muets* (1825) (*Mimography, or Essay on Sign Writing, Appropriate for Standardizing the Language of the Deaf*). In the latter work, he analyzed signs and concluded that it was possible to invent a script for sign language. He anticipated by one hundred twenty-five years the work of the American linguist William Stokoe. Stokoe's structural analyses were unique in their application to the sign language of deaf Americans.[15] But Bébian was too far ahead of his time, and the work was largely ignored.

Unfortunately, Bébian's skills in diplomacy were less impressive than his scholarly gifts. His intransigent character led to his dismissal from the Paris institute. Berthier worked hard to get him rehired, for he deeply admired his former professor. He believed that the talents of Bébian were almost equal to those of the Abbé de l'Épée, a great hero of Berthier's. When Bébian died in poverty, far from Paris, Berthier published a work devoted to him in 1839.[16] He was eager to rehabilitate the reputation of his friend, whom he saw as having been undervalued by society. He may also have been identifying with Bébian's angry activism and exploring how this stance both helped and hindered him in his life. Berthier himself had just spent a decade at war with the administration of the school in Paris.

In the early pages of the 1839 biography *Notice sur la Vie et les Ouvrages d'Auguste Bébian* (*Sketch of the Life and the Works of Auguste Bébian*), Berthier spoke of bringing Bébian's gifts out of the realm of oblivion. His intention was to portray Bébian's life and work, the monuments to a superior mind. According to Berthier, Bébian had demonstrated a lifetime devotion to deaf people, in spite of the many obstacles he faced, that made him worthy of the gratitude of humanity.

Roch-Ambroise-Auguste Bébian was born in 1789 in Pointe-à-Pitre, Guadeloupe. He was the oldest son of a businessman who was a member of a respected family on the island. His father sent him to the Abbé Sicard (his godfather) in France to be educated. He was boarded by the Abbé Jauffret, who later became the director of the Imperial School for the Deaf in St. Petersburg. In his schooling at the lycée Charlemagne, Bébian revealed two talents that were rare in the same person—imagination and patience.

Under the dual influences of Sicard and Jauffret, Bébian developed a vocation for deaf education. He attended classes, learned sign language, and became a close friend of young Laurent Clerc's. Bébian had a passion for, and understanding of, sign language and, early on, sensed that the signs developed by the Abbé de l'Épée and the Abbé Sicard were arbitrary and inadequate. Bébian's independent spirit was already manifesting itself, as was his intuitive understanding of deaf people. Berthier felt that Bébian's first work, *Essai sur les sourds-muets . . . (Essay on the Deaf . . .)* revealed a perfect understanding of the hearts and minds of deaf people.

As a teacher, Bébian believed that he was there for the students, to pay attention to them and their issues. Berthier signaled Bébian's respect for his students, who had previously been badly treated, even by the servants. Knowing this, the students often came to him when they had suffered an injustice. One young boy had been falsely accused of bad behavior and expelled from the school. He went tearfully to Bébian to ask him for his help. Bébian helped him to prove his innocence, and the student completed his courses and received a certificate.[17] Bébian was, in fact, such a committed teacher that he often used his salary for the benefit of the students.

Bébian had an admirable frankness and independence of character. He would not bend if he had a strong conviction. This, however, led him to criticize the administrators of the school frequently and harshly. Some of them did not take this very kindly and began to look for a reason to get rid of him. Without realizing it, Bébian fell into this trap, due to his own imprudent behavior. Even Berthier, his faithful friend and empathetic biographer, saw it as such, but he excused Bébian's actions as the excesses of a young man. Two incidents, in particular, forced Bébian to leave the school. One day, outraged by the behavior of an employee who he thought was corrupting the children, he fired him. This employee was viewed differently by the administration, who judged by the surface of things and saw that the employee took communion every Sunday.* Soon thereafter, an even more unfortunate event occurred. Bébian had long felt that the children were not clothed and fed well by the school's patrons and administrators. Surfacing unexpectedly during a visit by the duchess of Berry and the dukes of Levis and Montmoren-

---

* It is not known whether the employee was ever re-hired. The administration viewed Bébian as a rebel and fired him soon after this and another incident.

cy (the latter one of the school's administrators), in 1819 or 1820, Bébian offered the duchess some work written by the students. Predictably, she then asked to meet the students who had written the essays. It was impossible, Bébian said. The students were almost naked and not in a state to be introduced to her Royal Highness. They were even unable to take a walk outside for lack of clothing! Two days later he was asked to explain himself, but no explanation was accepted. Whether his criticisms were accurate or exaggerated, he had offended the duchess's sensibilities and embarrassed the school. He was vulnerable to his enemies now. He had to resign his position and leave the establishment. The students were in despair. They had lost their teacher and their best friend.[18]

The essential gift that Bébian brought to the deaf community at the school was a respect for their dignity. He wanted all of humanity to be equally respecting of deaf people and, above all, for deaf people to respect themselves. Berthier elegantly expressed this important idea about Bébian's stance toward his deaf friends: "les sourds-muets ne pouvaient oublier et n'oublieront jamais ses efforts pour relever en eux la dignité de l'homme" ("the deaf could not forget and will never forget his efforts to restore their human dignity").[19]

Bébian continued his work for deaf people although he was no longer employed at the school. He showed great perseverance, writing, giving personal counsel to deaf individuals and trying to calm their self-doubts. He received his former students in his home. He was offered the opportunity to be director of schools in St. Petersburg and New York, but his first love was France.

In 1830, when the bourgeois monarchy of Louis-Philippe began, Berthier thought that the new king might be favorably petitioned on behalf of Bébian. Berthier headed a small delegation of deaf artists and teachers, among them his friend Lenoir, who approached the king to ask for his support in bringing Bébian back to the Paris school. It had been nine years since Bébian had been fired. The king seemed willing to help the cause, but nothing happened because of the continuing ill will of the administrative council of the institute. Bébian had made some enemies and, as a result, was denied higher posts, but he did serve, for a time, as a teacher at the deaf school in Rouen, replacing the Abbé Huby, who had died. From all reports, he did well for the students there, but he was criticized for his administrative inadequacies. He was not much happier in Rouen than he had been in Paris. Further, the climate was increasingly difficult for Bébian, who became so ill that he finally had to leave.

He went back to Paris but could not improve his situation there. In fact, his presence awakened the old rancor and ill will, particularly when he joined the struggle to help deaf teachers fight against the rotation system. These intrigues, beginning around 1834, eventually led to Bébian's defeat. Finally, in desperation, for he was now quite poor, Bébian and his wife and son had to leave Paris in 1834 for Pointe-à-Pitre, Guadeloupe. Sadness followed him there. Bébian's son died a few years later. This loss affected him so deeply that Bébian, himself, died soon thereafter in 1839.

Berthier saw Bébian as a victim of ingratitude. He had given up everything for his work on behalf of deaf people: fortune, hope, and peace of mind. Sadly he died far from the people he had worked to validate, a fact that deeply troubled Berthier, for he would have wanted Bébian to sense the shared grief of his deaf friends in his last moments, As it was, he was on foreign soil. Nonetheless, Berthier emphasized that Bébian had accomplished a great task. He had been a liberator of deaf people and had managed this without help, without much money, and in spite of the obstacles that men, even more than circumstances, had placed before him.

In this analysis, Berthier was both friend and biographer, lamenting the loss of a dedicated supporter of the deaf community while saying that he lacked the skills to sufficiently commemorate such sacrifice. But in his portrait of Bébian, he also recognized a rebel whose outrageous behavior ended in personal destruction and diminished his contribution. Berthier understood that life posed the challenge of fighting for one's rights without awakening severe retribution. Bébian was an imperfect hero of the deaf community: his behavior was self-destructive and did not serve to diminish the divide between deaf and hearing people; if anything, it polarized the two. But he was unique in his dedication to, and acceptance by, deaf people, and for that, Berthier revered him.

IN HIS BIOGRAPHY of the Abbé de l'Épée, Berthier depicted a less problematical hero of deaf people. *L'Abbé de l'Épée, Sa Vie, Son Apostolat, Ses Travaux, Sa Lutte et Ses Succès . . .* (1852) (*The Abbé de l'Épée, His Life, His Apostolate, His Work, His Struggles and His Successes*) revealed the abbé as the "père spirituel" ("spiritual father") of deaf people and an early pioneer in the history of deaf education.[20] From the sixteenth to the early eighteenth centuries, the pioneers of deaf education were, with the exception of Étienne de Fay, hearing people, and they taught only children from rich families. They largely focused on teaching speech, and neither the teachers nor their students had contact with the linguistically deaf community.[21] Thus for many centuries, the majority of deaf people were victims of bias.

It was the abbé, in the eighteenth century, who was the first to say to the deaf community: "Et vous aussi, vous serez hommes!" ("And you, also, you will be men!").[22] The abbé respected the dignity of the deaf community and worked to diminish the barriers between deaf and hearing people. Deaf people reciprocated and gave back to the abbé and to society as a whole the fruits of the abbé's labor. Spirits and hearts were regenerated. Deaf people began to understand and to practice their religion, to share in the privileges and responsibilities of the community, and to cultivate the sciences and the arts. Berthier, beginning his work with these thoughts, gave us, early on, a thumbnail sketch of the abbé's unique contributions to the development of the deaf community.

Charles Michel de l'Épée was born on November 24, 1712. His father was architect of the king's buildings. His own studies at the Collège des Quatre Nations were for the clergy, but his Jansenism led him into difficulties, and he had to postpone becoming a priest. He then studied law but never had the same calling for it that he had to become a member of the clergy. He was finally ordained a priest in 1736, but because of his leanings toward Jansenism, he still had some limitations on his ability to practice his profession. He could not give sermons nor hear confessions. He passed his time productively, nonetheless, between his studies and his works of charity.

The theological principles of Jansenism emphasize predestination, deny free will, and state that human nature is basically flawed. People are more easily drawn to do evil than to do good. These principles were condemned as heretical by the Roman Catholic Church. The Abbé de l'Épée, who adhered to them in the early part of his career, was often at odds with the hierarchy of the church.

One day, the abbé came to a house on Fossés-St.-Victor Street, on some business of no great importance, according to Berthier. The mistress of the house was absent, and he was led into a room where her twin daughters were doing needlework, which they were watching attentively. The abbé addressed them but received no response. The mystery was solved when the mother appeared and said that her daughters were deaf. A Father Vanin, or Fanin (Berthier, the conscientious biographer, is uncertain of the spelling), had begun to teach the girls by means of engravings. But Father Vanin was now dead, and the despairing mother wondered who, if anyone, would teach her daughters. The abbé, moved by the deaf girls, realized he had discovered his vocation. He would find a way to instruct them.

Early on, he became convinced that sign language held the key to the education of the deaf. Berthier praised the abbé for seeing that sign offered a way to nurture the minds of deaf children and to replace hearing and speech. In his house on rue des Moulins he founded a school in which he taught numerous deaf children and held public lectures explaining his method. Berthier praised L'Epée for overcoming many obstacles in pursuing his new vocation. Many in his society still doubted that sign language could be used to educate deaf people. Philosophers and theologians questioned his methods sharply, while his contemporaries in deaf education argued with him and asked for proof.

To respond to all of these criticisms, and at the urging of friends who had wanted him to write about and discuss his method, the abbé gave demonstrations. These became quite famous during his time and were attended by a large public, including members of the royal family; Louis XVI, Joseph II, and Catherine II were among them. The abbé enjoyed demonstrating what his charges had learned. He was particularly happy that children who had previously been ignored or had caused their parents shame were now able to perform intellectual exercises on religious truths.

The Abbé de l'Épée's school was unique. Situated in Paris, the school offered all the advantages of the capital city. The abbé, in addition, did an excellent job of promoting it. In his public meetings, he demonstrated his teaching methods, hoping to gain sponsors, and he had many contacts with the nobility and royalty of his age. He attracted further attention by arguing forcefully with rivals concerning methodology and writing about his views on the instruction of the deaf. He set forth his ideas in *l'Institution des Sourds-Muets par la voie des signes méthodiques* (1774–1776) (*The Instruction of the Deaf through Methodical Signs*), in which he discussed his view that signs were the best means by which deaf people could learn to think and to reason.

A diverse public attended these meetings in the abbé's home. The room could hold only one hundred people. Often one found princes, ambassadors, judges, clergy, and people from Paris, from the provinces, and from foreign countries. The gazettes of the times, both national and international, provided the publicity that brought in these spectators. Much transpired on the stage as there were dictations, definitions of words, explanations of sentences, and responses to questions asked by the spectators. The students engaged the public for two hours. They were always enthusiastically applauded by the audience. It was a theatrical event popular with the public, who were curious to see the abbé and his work. Increasingly, the abbé was gaining fame both at home and abroad.

Beyond the theatrical aspect of these meetings, there was an educational purpose. Through them the public was beginning to cultivate a new attitude toward deaf people. As early as 1776, the abbé observed that these changes in attitude were already taking place. Previously deaf people had been viewed as objects of shame by friends and family. Some of the attendees at these public sessions became so intrigued that they created schools for the deaf themselves. The Abbé Sicard was a notable example. He attended the sessions, learning from the Abbé de l'Épée, and then returned to Bordeaux to become the director of the school for the deaf there in 1783.

Some years the abbé had as many as seventy students, recruited from many strata of society. He understood that for all of his students, visual-gestural communication in their classes, as well as in their daily lives, was of the greatest importance. He was the first hearing educator of deaf people to privilege a reading knowledge of French through signs over the spoken language. He was respected, even loved, by the deaf in all countries for this stance, which validated their sign language, reflecting its centrality in their lives.[23] It is probably largely through his efforts and influence that the existence of deaf people as a segment of society began to be recognized at the end of the eighteenth century.

Berthier, himself, had a passion for sign language and its possibilities, calling it "cette langue sublime, universelle, basée sur la nature et la raison" ("that sublime, universal language, based on nature and reason").[24] He credited the Abbé de l'Épée for his support of sign language but felt that he did not have sufficient faith in the possibilities of sign in and of itself. In order to teach his students written French, L'Epée used signs in French word order, and he created signs for French grammatical constructions that did not exist in French Sign Language. He called this system "methodical signs." Berthier did not endorse the abbé's use of methodical signs.

Berthier, thus, acknowledged the possibility that his hero could err. Another problematical issue for Berthier was the abbé's role in the episode of the Count of Solar. The abbé became involved in trying to find the origins of a young, deaf boy who had been abandoned on the highway in 1773. The boy, according to Berthier, was either the victim of a terrible prejudice or of a criminal act. The abbé came to believe that the boy, whom he called Joseph, was the son of the Count of Solar. L'Epée tried to regain the boy's title and heritage for him, against warring elements in the society. The child, himself, through descriptive signs, had led the abbé to believe in his noble origins. He described wealthy parents, a deceased father, an elegant home and garden, and a masked criminal leading him away from his home to the devastating destination of the highway. Others continued to insist that Joseph was not the count and that the real count had died in 1774. The tribunal finally ruled against Joseph in 1792, reversing several earlier judgments in his favor.

Joseph's death was as shrouded in mystery as his life. One version had it that, having enlisted in the army, he died in combat, not hearing the signal to retreat. Another version of the story was that he died in the army hospital. Given this tragic outcome, had the abbé done the right thing? Had he been overly zealous and overly gullible? Later evidence seemed to cast doubt on Joseph's presumed identity as the count. But Berthier maintained that the abbé's desire to defend the rights of all of his deaf adoptive sons was pure. L'Epée viewed Joseph as a victim and firmly believed he was the count; consequently, he had to do all that he could to support him.

This episode represents the only time the abbé assumed the activist role that we saw Bébian assume throughout his life. The abbé's previous strategies for bridging the gulf between hearing and deaf people involved education, for both communities, to aid them in seeing the value of understanding one another: he wanted to teach his students to be good citizens and good Catholics and to educate the larger public about deaf people through his writings and demonstrations. The Solar case tended to polarize all who were involved in it and all those who heard about it.

The ongoing trial connected to this case had added to the now aged and ailing abbé's fatigue. He died on September 23, 1789, at the age of seventy-seven, surrounded by his students. Before his death, he had received word from the National Assembly that the government would care for his children and his establishment. The assembly kept its word. On April 6, 1790, the Abbé Sicard, one of the Abbé de l'Épée's protégés, director of the school for the deaf in Bordeaux, was chosen to be his successor by the highest dignitaries in the government. The two schools, in Paris and in Bordeaux, became national institutions in July and September of 1791.

In the conclusion of his biography of the abbé, Berthier spoke of his desire to assure a "post life" for the Abbé de l'Épée. The abbé had to be memorialized through monuments and other artistic ventures and through celebrations. Above all, his work in creating and supporting the deaf community had to be continued. His was a unique contribution. Berthier could see faults in the abbé's endeavors, but Berthier revered the Abbé de l'Épée more as a distant idol than as a human being, which poses the question as to whether this work is hagiography or biography.

Early in the biography, Berthier tells the story of St. Francis, which seems to invite comparison with the life and contributions of the Abbé de l'Épée that are sketched in this work. In 1604, during a stay at la Roche, St. Francis accepted a poor deaf man into his service. He was touched by the man's situation and ignored an observation on the part of someone on his staff that the man would be an expense and offer him nothing in return. St. Francis countered that the man offered him the opportunity to be charitable. St. Francis also instructed the deaf man in the mysteries of faith and taught him to confess. He apparently taught him love and gratitude, as well, for the deaf man died of grief soon after St. Francis died.

The Abbé de l'Épée, too, offered charity, instruction, and validation to deaf people and would be mourned by them upon his death. If the faults recognized by Berthier and discussed in his writings on the abbé prevent us from seeing the abbé as a saint, we can perceive that he, nonetheless, had taken as his model the selfless dedication of the most saintly lives, and Berthier saw and reported this.

❧

L'EPÉE'S SELFLESSNESS deeply contrasts with the self-serving nature of Berthier's next biographical subject, Roch-Ambroise Cucurron, the Abbé Sicard (1742–1822). This work, published in 1873, recounts the personal and professional life and adventures of the Abbé Sicard.[25] The lengthy essay has appended to it two shorter but equally interesting portraits of the Abbé Sicard's most gifted students, Jean Massieu and Laurent Clerc.

Sicard was born in 1742 in Foussert, a small village in Languedoc. He was taken under the wing of the Archbishop of Bordeaux, Monseigneur Champion de Cicé, who assigned him the directorship of a school for the deaf in Bordeaux. Before assuming this task, Sicard went to study with the Abbé de l'Épée in 1785, a year before he actually became the director of the Bordeaux school. Sicard actively recruited numerous deaf students for his school in Bordeaux. The most gifted of these was Jean Massieu. Massieu was from a large family and had been a shepherd until a friend of the family's had brought him to Sicard's school, when Massieu was thirteen. He became Sicard's favorite student, and Massieu, in turn, was completely devoted to his teacher.

Upon the death of the Abbé de l'Épée, Sicard persuaded the revolutionaries that there should be a competition for the directorship of the school in Paris. (The Abbé de l'Épée had indicated his preference for the Abbé Masse before he died.) Sicard's idea was accepted and he competed against Masse and Salvan (Salvan was a priest who directed a school for the deaf in Auvergne). He won easily with the aid of Massieu, who astounded the jury with the brilliance of his answers. On April 6, 1790, Sicard was named to the coveted post. It was under Sicard's direction that Berthier's schooling took place.

On July 21, 1791, the National Institute for the Deaf was officially founded. The intention was to create a revolutionary utopia, offering education to all; soon after the institute's creation, blind people were sent to share this facility on Célestins Street with deaf students. This arrangement would last for a little less than three years, for the notion of a utopia would soon be eroded by the profound jealousy and anger that developed between Sicard and the principal instructor of the blind, Valentin Haüy.

Sicard was a cleric and a royalist, while Haüy was a layman and a revolutionary. From the beginning of their sharing of the facility, there were serious conflicts due to their beliefs and their respective competitive natures. The two vied with one another for resources. If Sicard went to the National Assembly with his students to gain some benefit, Haüy would go as well, and he had his students perform "The Marseillaise" (the French national anthem) before this same group to get an equal sum of money or equal benefit. They both encouraged their students to compete with one another.

Finally, moved by an escalating anger, Haüy had Sicard arrested in August of 1792. Sicard was accused of being a counterrevolutionary because of his religious principles. Showing significantly more maturity than either of their teachers, the deaf and blind children united to beg for Sicard's release. The delegation of students, led by Massieu, petitioned the legislative assembly on his behalf. In a touching and powerful address, Massieu spoke of Sicard's dedication to his students and the deaf students' feeling of loss at their director's imprisonment. He presented Sicard as their "father," insisting that he had taught them to espouse the principles of the revolution.

Sicard later suggested that Massieu had said that the deaf students were unable to function without him. In actual fact, Massieu and his classmates had behaved in an admirably autonomous way, taking the initiative to petition the assembly in support of their teacher and director. It was clear that they needed Sicard less than he thought.

In spite of the petitions of the students, Sicard remained in prison for an extended period of time and was almost executed on several occasions. At one point, all the men around him were being killed, and Sicard had no doubt that he would be next. A clock maker, citizen Monnot, ran to investigate the news his son had given him of the continuing massacre in the prisons. Familiar with Sicard's work, Monnot bravely stepped in front of Sicard, who was about to be pierced with a sword.

He told the revolutionaries that they had to kill him (Monnot) before they killed Sicard. This man is the father and teacher of the deaf, he informed them. The immediate response of the crowd was rather unpromising: "C'est égal, c'est un aristocrate" ("It doesn't matter; he's still an aristocrat") the crowd roared back.[26] But none were willing to slay Monnot, who was a respected member of the Civil Committee, and Sicard escaped execution.

Although he escaped death, the abbé had many terrifying experiences. During his imprisonment, the abbé's cell companions went mad. One gave the abbé a knife and asked him to kill him. Another tried to hang himself with his own clothing. The abbé overheard a man driving a carriage say that the abbé was to be killed that same afternoon. Only the frequent intervention of friends prevented the assassination of Sicard.

Upon his release, Sicard was advised not to return to the school yet but to seek shelter with another clock maker named Lacombe, who had done much to support the abbé during his detention. It was there that Sicard received his first visit from Massieu. The latter had refused food and drink and had not slept at all during Sicard's incarceration. He was completely distraught. One day more, Berthier told us, and Massieu would have died of hunger and pain. These feelings of affection were at least somewhat shared by Sicard, who had earlier on, when he was still imprisoned, left his watch for Massieu as a keepsake when he believed he was about to be executed.

By 1796 Sicard's career began to flourish again. He was a teacher at the National Lycée and occupied a chair at the prestigious École normale supérieure. Sicard's problems with the revolutionaries continued, however. Fortunately, he was sustained by many friends, particularly Jean Massieu. The latter was so devoted to his teacher that he offered to share his small salary with him when Sicard was forced to hide from his radical enemies. Not surprisingly, Sicard broke completely with Haüy upon his return to the Paris institute, and within two years, the deaf students had separated from the blind ones and had moved into the former Saint-Magloire Seminary on Saint-Jacques Street, where the school still stands in somewhat renovated form today. It was here that the Abbé Sicard did a great deal of his thinking and writing about deaf people.

Though he was proud of aspects of the abbé's work, Berthier spoke of absurdities, nonetheless, in some of Sicard's views of the deaf. In his *Cours d'instruction d'un sourd-muet de naissance . . .* (1800) (*Course of Instruction for a Person Born Deaf*), Sicard concluded that before an education that linked him to society, a deaf person "c'est un être parfaitement nul dans la société, un automate vivant, une statue." ("He is a being of absolutely no value in society, a living automaton, a statue.").[27] In fact, Sicard placed the deaf person below animals, for they had instincts.

Outraged by these comments, Berthier said, correctly, that the stupidity of the notion that an as-yet-untaught deaf person was beneath an animal might just cause a person to shrug his shoulders. But that such a statement came from a deaf educator rightfully caused great indignation to Berthier and to all the students in the school. Berthier pointed out that any deaf child ten years or older who lived among other people had learned from them how to communicate, albeit imperfectly, even without formal education. So the deaf person in the untrained, animal state discussed by Sicard did not exist.

Sicard revised his thinking in his *Théorie des Signes . . .* (1823) (*Theory of Signs . . .*). He spoke in this work of the communicative soul of the young deaf person who had formed ideas based on his perception of external objects and found that he was no worse off than the young hearing person who has just left his parents for school. But this later work was less widely read than the earlier one, and Berthier believed that the damage was never completely undone. Nor did Berthier feel that Sicard appreciated the full value of sign language for teaching the deaf. Sicard's knowledge was limited to methodical signs. He had not lived long enough with his students to get a sense of the possibilities offered by their natural language. Bébian, rather than the Abbé Sicard, developed the important idea that deaf students needed to be taught in their own language.

Nonetheless, Sicard had many friends among the powerful who offered their support to the deaf institute and often came to visit and observe the performances of the students, as had been done at the time of the Abbé de l'Épée. Such patronage, of course, was of great service to the Institution. Among the famous visitors was Pope Pius VII, who listened attentively to a discourse from Sicard, received compliments from the children, and then toured the institute, visiting the printing press, the workshops, and the dormitories. Among the more astounding assertions made by Sicard to the pontiff was that he (Sicard) had managed to overcome all problems related to the education of the deaf and could take any religious, moral, and scientific thought and explain it to his students. At least some people, during his time, shared this favorable view of himself, for Sicard received the medal of the Legion of Honor in 1814.

In spite of his continuing successes, the abbé had been affected by the events of the Reign of Terror and often fell into periods of silence and depression. The victim of intrigues until the end of his life, Sicard was accused of supporting Louis XVIII and of expressing opinions hostile to the emperor. Fearing for his life again, Sicard left Paris for London, taking Massieu and Clerc with him. In spite of the anger of the minister of the interior, Carnot, Sicard did not return with his students until Napoleon was overthrown.

As Sicard aged, the number of intriguing solicitors, flatterers, and courtiers began to multiply around him. Already weakened by his continuing political struggles, the abbé was affected by this proliferation of enemies, all of whom were trying to control his mind and spirit. Berthier noted that Sicard became almost childlike. He had never been good with money, but in later years, he lost his fortune completely, including thirty thousand francs (thirty years of wages) that Massieu had loaned him and that would never be repaid. He was, according to Berthier, too naive to suspect others of having bad motives and thus fell prey to many schemes.

Strangely, he was strong enough to resist pressure from those around him who told him to leave his post. He insisted that he would not do so, saying that he planned to work until the end of his life. When he felt close to his end, he wrote to the Abbé Gondelin, from the Bordeaux school, intending to leave him his directorship of the school. But it was the Abbé Périer, founder and director of the deaf school in Rodez, who followed Sicard as the school's director.

As he approached the conclusion of his narrative, Berthier shifted direction. Perhaps thinking he had set out for the reader too many of the foibles of Sicard, he proceeded to speak of his personal gratitude toward him for all the kindnesses he had done on his behalf. Admitted to the institute at eight, Berthier shared the "pain intellectuel" ("intellectual bread")[28] of Sicard throughout his childhood and youth. Among the acts of kindness most remembered by Berthier was the time Sicard introduced Berthier to Louis XVIII and allowed him to present a portrait of Henri IV to him.

But it was Jean Massieu and Laurent Clerc, Sicard's best students, who became Berthier's mentors and models at the institute. Jean Massieu was the first deaf teacher at the Paris institute, and he did not leave it until 1823. Laurent Clerc left for America in 1816, at the request of Thomas Hopkins Gallaudet, in order to establish a school for the deaf in America in which students would be taught in sign language. Both Clerc and Massieu had a profound effect on Berthier, who clearly took pleasure in chronicling their lives.

His biographical sketches of them, however, are appended to the biography of the Abbé Sicard and, although written with respect, affection, and Berthier's usual care, are less lengthy and developed than that of their mentor. Did Berthier know less about their lives, particularly the later years, because both had left the Paris institute? Or, a more disturbing thought, had he been infected, on some level, by Sicard's self-aggrandizement and denigration of his deaf students? Berthier's structuring of this collective biography, in any case, mirrors two lives that benefited from, but eventually needed to separate from, a hardworking but flawed, self-serving mentor.

Jean Massieu, the older of the two disciples, was born in 1772 in the village of Semens to poor parents who already had five other deaf children. Massieu spent his early years watching over a flock of sheep for his parents. Even at this juncture, although he was uneducated, he showed a native intelligence. He counted the sheep on his fingers, and when the number surpassed ten, he marked it on his stick and began counting all over again.

He showed a passion for education in his early years, approaching his father and showing him with gestures that he wanted to go to school and learn to read and to write. His father, sad at his son's request that seemed impossible to satisfy, tried to help him to understand that his unusual situation did not allow for that. In the meantime, young Massieu asked his family to uncork his ears as one would uncork a bottle. He thought that this might be a simple way to eliminate this obstacle. Determined, Massieu took a book and went to school on his own. He opened a book in class, tried to scan the pages and moved his lips in imitation of the hearing children. The teacher was both unable and unwilling to help him and Massieu was forced to leave the classroom, struck by feelings of frustration and powerlessness. This could well have been the end of his efforts to achieve formal schooling.

But in a fortunate turn of events, a charitable citizen of the area, Monsieur de Puymaurin was touched by Massieu and the situation in which he found himself and, sensing Massieu's innate talents, brought him to the Institute for the Deaf in Bordeaux, currently under the direction of the Abbé Sicard. At thirteen, Massieu was accepted and began his studies there. His progress soon justified the opinion that others had of his potential, particularly Monsieur de Puymaurin.

Massieu was Sicard's favorite student. So, upon the death of the Abbé de l'Épée, when Sicard became director of the Paris Institute, he took Massieu with him. It was, in large measure, Massieu's brilliance that had helped him to attain this, his last and best post. In Paris, Massieu began to develop professionally and soon was earning a salary that he generously planned to share with his family: "Je pourrai assurer enfin du pain à la vieillesse de ma mère" ("I shall finally be able to guarantee my mother bread in her old age").[29]

In a choice that was rare for a deaf person of his times, Jean Massieu wrote an autobiographical statement. It focused on his early years and was written at the request of a person curious about his beginnings.[30]He noted his place of birth and the fact that his father had died in January of 1791 but that his mother was still alive. He explained that there were three deaf girls and three deaf boys in the family. He was in spiritual darkness until he was thirteen years and nine months old. He managed to communicate with family members through gestures but they were not those of educated deaf people.

He saw animals (oxen, horses, donkeys, pigs, dogs, cats, he specified) and other objects and, after looking at them carefully, he was able to remember them. But he yearned for school, wanting to learn to read and to write. And then, clearly telling a story that pained him, Massieu recounted the episode of his trip to the school and his efforts to get an unkind teacher to help him to become literate. The harsh teacher, duplicating the reception that Massieu got from all of the neighborhood children, chased him away, as you would a dog.

In his early years, his father made him pray, but Massieu had no conception of a God who created heaven and earth; he adored the sky only and saw nothing beyond it. Without the Abbé Sicard, Massieu once said, his spirit would have remained undeveloped. It was Monsieur de Puymaurin who brought him to the abbé, and in the space of four years (the number of years that had passed at the time he framed these remarks) he had become quite literate, reading and writing well and answering questions: "Je suis devenu comme les entendants-parlants" ("I became like hearing-speaking people").[31] In fact, Massieu's answers to questions, as well as the definitions he offered in the public demonstrations of the Abbé Sicard, electrified those who came to observe them. He defined "gratitude" as the memory of the heart, to give one example.[32] But his profound elevated answers and definitions contrasted with the childlike, simple style of his letters and familiar conversation. And Berthier sadly commented that because of this, some concluded that an individual with deafness could not attain the educational level of a hearing person.

Berthier challenged this view and reexamined the question. Did Sicard have some responsibility for these deficits? He wanted his students to develop formal skills and neglected to teach the less formal ones, those less likely to be exhibited in public. But shouldn't Sicard have worked more on developing a means of everyday communication that would link deaf people with the hearing? It was Sicard's job, he felt, to lower the barriers between deaf and hearing people for Massieu, for all of his students.

Massieu had behavioral quirks along with the gaps in his education outlined by Berthier. His demeanor, Berthier told us, suggested that this man who frequented royalty was a stranger to civilization. He dressed in a somewhat careless way and was naive, hiding nothing from his friends, confiding his anxieties and consulting his friends not only about simple things but about the most serious matters. This was unacceptable to Berthier, who had a more formal idea of professionalism, feeling it was linked with greater personal privacy.

Massieu had a childlike passion for certain objects. He loved golden keys and watches and wore as many as four or five little clocks at a time. He looked at them constantly and often showed them to his friends, expecting their admiration, as well. He was even more obsessive about books, buying them constantly, everywhere he went. He carried them about in his pockets, in his arms, in his hands, and after having showed them to everyone, he traded them in for others. He was generally good-natured about these foibles and would tolerate a certain amount of teasing, but occasionally he would become brusque if he became too offended.

Berthier observed that Massieu had many good qualities that compensated for his small faults. He was an excellent friend and remained grateful for kindnesses his friends showed him. This was certainly true in his relationship with Sicard. He had said of their friendship: "Lui et moi . . . nous sommes deux barres de fer forgées ensemble" ("He and

I . . . we are two iron bars soldered together").[33] This devotion on the part of Massieu remained constant, even when he discovered, upon the death of Sicard, that there was not enough money left in Sicard's possession to repay Massieu for an earlier loan to his teacher. This money borrowed and never returned represented thirty years of wages that Massieu had saved and that were now lost.

Partly out of financial necessity and partly out of a desire to create a new life, Massieu went to Rodez, at the request of the Abbé Périer. Périer encouraged the social/familial development of Massieu's personality. At his urging, Massieu married a hearing woman in Rodez and had two hearing children. When the Abbé Périer left for Paris, he placed Massieu in charge of his school in Rodez.

After the death of the Abbé Périer, Monsieur Vanackère, a wealthy bookseller in Lille, urged Massieu to return to that city. Massieu had been there in 1820 to lecture on the art of teaching the deaf. Massieu had been well received in that city and decided that he'd go to work in Lille. A school was founded there in 1835, and Massieu became its director. There were only ten deaf students at first, but by 1839, the number had jumped to forty. The school was well organized; it was placed under the inspection and supervision of a commission presided over by the mayor of the city. Monsieur Vanackère served on this commission and was one of its most dedicated members.

There developed between Massieu and Vanackère a deep friendship and mutual respect, which led to an excellent working relationship. Vanackère was for Massieu a guide, a source of emotional support, and a counselor who worked tirelessly alongside him. Massieu, in turn, offered his talent and ingenuity in teaching the deaf. Under their joint leadership, the establishment became a source of pride to the community.

Massieu also developed, to some extent, as a writer, although Berthier was critical of his skills in this area. Massieu began work on his *Mémoires* (*Memoirs*), fragments of which were published in a local newspaper, *Le Nord*, in 1838. Berthier found them to be unsophisticated. Massieu wrote largely about Sicard's imprisonment during the Revolution and about his efforts to support his teacher and to get him released. Nonetheless, these *Mémoires* constituted a second effort at autobiographical writing on the part of Massieu, when few models of such writing were available to deaf people.

Sadly, not too long after this, Massieu's memory began to fail, and he entered the last phase of his life. He was accorded the title of honorary director of the school until the end of his days, and he was cared for by the brothers of Saint-Gabriel and the sisters of La Sagesse until his death on July 23, 1846, at the age of seventy-four. Tributes to Massieu upon his death revealed the community's respect and admiration for his work in Lille. The ties between Massieu and Vanackère were touchingly reaffirmed, as well. Vanackère, who had predeceased Massieu, had indicated that he wanted his friend's tomb to be placed near his own. These wishes were followed, with no one doubting the depth of the friendship between the two men.

Karacostas saw Massieu as the deaf alter ego of Sicard.[34] The connections between the two were undeniable. Massieu helped Sicard obtain his appointment at the deaf school in Paris, and he continued to shine in the frequent public meetings led by Sicard for the benefit of the school. He saved his teacher from almost certain death numerous times during the French Revolution. What Massieu received in return was more problematical. It is true that Sicard offered this boy from a poor family his first opportunity to be educated, and no doubt this facilitated Massieu's intellectual and moral development. But Sicard took advantage of Massieu's reserves of energy, goodwill, and even his financial resources. It was only after Sicard's death that Massieu found a better mentor and more equal relationship with Vanackère, who encouraged him to hone his skills as teacher, director, and writer. This relationship was much more personally satisfying and less stressful. Throughout his life, however, Massieu served as a great link between the worlds of deaf and hearing people, fulfilling that role for Sicard, Périer, and Vanackère.

Laurent Clerc, the second of Sicard's disciples, came into the world in 1785 in la Balme, near Lyon. He had a triple infirmity: he was deaf, and unable to speak or smell. But nature compensated him for these deficits in other ways. He was not yet twelve when he began attending the Abbé Sicard's school. His progress there was even more remarkable than Massieu's. He, like Massieu, was called upon to demonstrate the effectiveness of the establishment in the public demonstrations that took place at least twice a month. His answers to questions were as well received as those of his classmate. He had, in addition, certain qualities that the idiosyncratic Massieu lacked. He had polite and engaging manners and kept good company. He was, according to Berthier, a true gentleman.

Further, he was modest, in spite of his own significant intellectual gifts, and generous in his praise of others, particularly Massieu, to whom he was often compared, as the following episode indicates. Once Sicard sent Clerc to ask an associate in the French Academy for the return of a book that he had loaned him. The illustrious academician decided to test Clerc's reputation for intelligence and asked him challenging questions of a metaphysical nature. Struck by Clerc's excellent answers, Sicard's colleague told him how much he admired him. Clerc told him the truly impressive experience would have come from questioning Massieu and receiving his responses.

Clerc knew several languages: French, English, American Sign Language (ASL), and French Sign Language (LSF). He thought all deaf people should know the sign languages of their individual communities and the written languages of their countries. He had, then, a more inclusive linguistic view than many of his predecessors. He spent his life very much connected to the deaf community, first in France, then in America. He saw deafness as a way of being in the world, not as a handicap. He clearly rejected oralism and favored signs, signing beautifully and believing that sign language was the medium for teaching the deaf and for communication between and among deaf people.[35]

Clerc, in fact, often enjoyed interpreting for deaf colleagues when important visitors arrived, and he wrote when others needed a secretary. A Hungarian deaf man, a former student of the Deaf Institute in Vienna, founded by Joseph II and based on the methods of the Abbé de l'Épée, had come to Paris, looking for a job as an engraver. He had debts and needed to find work, he told Clerc. Clerc offered to accompany the unfortunate artist to the Austrian embassy, near the court of France, to explain the situation to the ambassador.

When Clerc broached the subject to Sicard, the latter questioned his ability to communicate with the diplomat. How could he possibly do this? Clerc, more self-confident and less mesmerized by Sicard than Massieu, reproached his teacher: "Comment? . . . vous, mon cher maître, le grand instituteur des sourds-muets, vous me le demandez!" ("What? . . . you, my dear teacher, the great instructor of the deaf, you are asking me this!")[36] Clerc went on to explain that he would translate into written French for the ambassador the signs of the poor Hungarian deaf artist. Of course, Clerc continued, an ambassador from Austria to the court of France would certainly know French. But it was Clerc's abilities that Sicard was questioning, revealing again Sicard's flawed understanding of and belief in even the best of his students.

But Clerc was about to embark on an adventure that would lead him away from this very imperfect mentor. Soon after Clerc had returned from England where he and Massieu had accompanied Sicard, they were sought out by a young Protestant minister, Thomas Hopkins Gallaudet. Gallaudet had been sent to Europe by some families of deaf children who were eager to establish a school for the deaf in America, where, as yet, none existed. The only option for wealthy American parents was to send their deaf children to one of several schools in England or France.

Thomas Gallaudet had the funds to travel to England to learn the methodology used in teaching deaf children there. But in England, one family controlled the five schools for the deaf in the country, and they kept their method secret. Gallaudet could have access to the schools only if he paid a high fee, which he was unable to do. He had spent a frustrating year trying, in vain, to get access to the classrooms of the deaf children schooled in England.

One day in London, Gallaudet observed a demonstration given by Sicard and his two talented students. Impressed by the knowledge of the deaf students, Gallaudet approached Sicard, who invited him to Paris, an invitation that Gallaudet accepted. Once in Paris, Gallaudet studied with both Massieu and Clerc to develop his sign language and observed Clerc's classes. He stayed in Paris for three months, revealing to his French hosts his personal charm and intellectual capabilities. Mindful of Clerc's gifts and his own relatively slow mastery of signs, Gallaudet asked Clerc to accompany him to the United States and become his associate there in his plan to establish a school for the deaf in America.

Clerc was torn and found the decision very difficult. He was very much a Frenchman. He wrote French easily, loved to read in French, and loved his country's history, architecture, and food. (According to Harlan Lane, frogs' legs were a particular favorite!) It was difficult for him to leave France for America, but he felt it was his mission to do so. He wrote about his conflicted feelings in his journal: "Je ne veux pas partir, mais je pense que j'y suis obligé" ("I don't want to leave, but I think that I have to").[37]

Clerc had to deal not only with his own hesitations but with the wrath of Sicard. Upset at the impending loss of his best teacher, Sicard told Clerc that if he went to America, he would burn in hell. (This was because there were not yet any Catholic churches in America!)[38] This could not have been easy for Clerc to take, because he took his religion, Catholicism, seriously and was viewed by most around him as a man much given to reflection and prayer. But in the same way that he was able to confront Sicard when his teacher questioned his talents, he refused to allow these alarming words to prevent him from deciding to go with Gallaudet on the long journey to America. The goal seemed noble to him, and perhaps he welcomed independence from this rather irrational despot who ruled the French deaf institute. Berthier added in his discussion of Clerc's departure that it was made somewhat easier for him in that Clerc had always felt somewhat insulted by the poor pay that he had received at the Paris institute.[39]

The trip to America took fifty-three days at that time. During the journey, Gallaudet helped Clerc to improve his English, and Clerc continued to teach sign language to Gallaudet. They established a fine relationship that endured through the years. Once they arrived in Hartford, Connecticut, the two traveled throughout the region to raise funds. Gallaudet introduced Clerc, saying deaf children could be educated as well as hearing children. Clerc then signed his own lecture, with Gallaudet as interpreter. All who heard them were impressed and were quick to support and contribute to this new venture: the establishment of a school for the deaf in the New World.

Clerc had left France in 1816 and worked at the American Asylum in Hartford, Connecticut, from 1817 to 1858. He had a happy life in America, earning the friendship and esteem of all around him. He was a highly effective teacher who taught both hearing and deaf in the Hartford School. The hearing people were most often teachers of the deaf who wanted to learn sign language and teaching methodology. His students greatly admired him. He married a deaf woman and had six hearing children. Gallaudet similarly married a deaf American of whom he was proud, and they had eight children, all hearing.

In addition to having to negotiate the boundaries between the hearing and deaf, Clerc had the additional challenge of coming to terms with his lifelong love of France and his past life there, along with his developing new life in America. He traveled back to France in 1820, 1825, and 1847, Berthier told us.[40] He would combine business and discussion about his new venture in America with visits to friends. In his last letter to Berthier, his former student, in 1856, the two lives of Clerc connected. He wrote a letter of introduction for his friend Madame Batler, who was traveling to Paris with her daughters. (Her husband, Jean Batler, had been a member of the board of the Hartford School.) Clerc wanted her to see the institution where he had been brought up, the classroom where he taught, the room he occupied, and the room where he took his meals. He especially wanted her to meet the other deaf teachers. He was, of course, being courteous to the wife and daughters of a board member in Hartford, feeling pride in his intellectual roots and his former deaf colleagues in Paris, but he was also, I believe, creating a link between the two lives that he had lived. Clerc retired soon after, in 1858. He died in 1869, at the age of eighty-three, having earned the gratitude and respect of all who had known him in both countries.

The association between Gallaudet and Clerc was reminiscent of the relationship that Massieu finally found with Vanackère after the Abbé Sicard's death. It can be argued that it was a more equal one since Clerc had a more highly developed, or at least a more resilient, personality than Massieu. Clerc shared with Gallaudet the language and the methods used to teach the deaf at the Paris institute. He was, further, an excellent model of what a deaf person could become. Gallaudet, in turn, gave Clerc his friendship and the opportunity to pursue his professional goals. It was an impressive collaboration between a deaf man and a hearing man, and Berthier clearly enjoyed chronicling it.

In the course of his professional life and career, Jean-Ferdinand Berthier experienced several stages of development in his attitudes toward bridging the gap between deaf and hearing people. His first stage may be seen as prepolitical, although he clearly believed that sign language was superior to speech (reflected in the drawing "The Man with a Serpent") and demonstrated a strong commitment to the deaf community. But his major interest at this time was in the field of education. With the help of Bébian, he secured a post at the deaf institute in Paris and devoted himself to teaching his students.

By the early 1830s, in response to the strong oralist orientation of the Institut National de Jeunes Sourds where Berthier taught, Berthier became politicized and, to some extent, remained so, although the deaf teachers regained their full status at the institute by 1836. Berthier was now acutely aware of the vulnerable position of deaf people in society. In the years to follow, he founded numerous social and political organizations to support the needs and rights of deaf people and to celebrate deaf culture. He passionately defended sign language as the best means of educating deaf children, and he spoke against the hearing society's many misconceptions about deaf people, even on the part of those who educated the deaf. Here Berthier was angrily targeting the Abbé Sicard, who was less sensitive to the talents and needs of the deaf than his predecessor, the Abbé de l'Épée.

It seems, indeed, that Berthier had arrived at a position of fairly complete polarization concerning deaf and hearing people. Although that may have been the case, at this same stage in his life, a subtle dynamic can be seen working itself out through his biographical writings, in which Berthier first expressed, then gradually defused, his anger, finding his way "home" to a more balanced view: the need for deaf and hearing people to coexist in a more creative manner. Thus, he can be said to have used his writing as a means of self-healing.

Berthier's early work, exemplified by his biography of Bébian, *Notice sur la Vie et les Ouvrages d'Auguste Bébian* (1839), revealed a strongly militant stance. Berthier clearly identified with his bold teacher, Bébian, who was a rebel, unafraid to criticize a powerful school administration or the methodical signs used by the Abbé de l'Épée and the Abbé Sicard. Berthier, the biographer, injected himself into the narrative to inform the reader that his sympathies lay with this activist-separatist who had the courage to defy an unfair system that had victimized him. But Bébian's actions were extreme and led to his firing from an institution he revered, to a greater division between the deaf and hearing people around him, and, most painfully for Berthier, to a separation from his deaf friends at the time of his final illness and death, as financial circumstances forced him to leave Paris for Guadeloupe.

By 1852, however, in writing the life of the Abbé de l'Épée, Berthier could see possibilities other than separation between deaf and hearing people. In a moving tribute, Berthier noted that the abbé was the first to acknowledge the humanity of deaf people. Through the abbé's good work, barriers between deaf and hearing people began to come down. Berthier stated his belief that if the education of the deaf continued to improve, deaf people would increasingly accept their responsibilities to the society at large and open their hearts and minds to hearing people. Thus we see that Berthier, earlier a separatist, is beginning to express a desire for, and a belief in, the need for reconnection to the larger society.

The same trend intensified in his later work, notably in his two studies of Massieu and Clerc, appended to the biography of the Abbé Sicard, *L'Abbé Sicard* (1873). Berthier used a number of strategies for working out the differences between hearing and deaf people. In the studies of Massieu and Clerc, we see collaborations between hearing and deaf male protagonists as mentors or friends. Clerc, more aware of Sicard's limitations than Massieu, left his apprenticeship with him for a more satisfying one with Gallaudet. The relationship between the two men soon became one of equals. On the trip back to America, there was already an exchange of sign language and English lessons, and in the United States, they worked together to establish the school in Hartford.

Massieu had a more complex relationship with Sicard, whom he worshipped. Less sophisticated than Clerc, he was less able to protect himself from Sicard's shortcomings, or even to acknowledge that he had any. It is true that Sicard had opened doors for Massieu, who had been raised in poverty. Massieu had more than reciprocated, however. He had tried to protect Sicard from the excesses of the French Revolution. He had even loaned Sicard significant sums of money, money that was never repaid.

Fortunately, later in life, Massieu had a more reciprocal friendship with another hearing man, a wealthy bookseller from Lille named Vanackère, who recognized Massieu's gifts and urged him to come to Lille and to establish a school for the deaf there. The school flourished, as did their friendship. Vanackère offered Massieu wise counsel and respect. It was a creative mentorship, less flawed than the one offered him by Sicard.

In these portraits of the lives of two of Sicard's students, Berthier showed the reader how they achieved less marginal positions in mainstream society with the aid of hearing mentors. It is my belief that, in so doing, Berthier was charting a similar course for himself.

Thus, I can outline three stages of development concerning Berthier's attitude toward bridging the gulf between deaf and hearing people. A preactivist phase signaled the earliest stage of his career. Between 1829 and 1832, he became politicized as a result of the temporary loss of his job. The last stage was slower in developing, seemingly beginning around 1852 and continuing at least until 1880, and possibly beyond. This was the period during which he indicated a desire for reconciliation between deaf and hearing people. This reconciliation may have been aided, in part, by the healing effects of dealing with his own anger with hearing people through the medium of his biographical portraits of others.

Did this more positive phase remain with him, at least in some measure, after the results of the Congress of Milan, and its advocacy of oralism in teaching the deaf? His silence and withdrawal from the fray are puzzling, but in 1880 he was an aging man, threatened by a developing blindness. We can only hope that he kept the faith that sign language and deaf culture would once again flourish. His own experience with the deaf institute in Paris demonstrated that it only took a few heroes like himself to bring about constructive change.

4 Yvonne Pitrois

A Journey from Darkness to Light

YVONNE PITROIS (1880–1937) was born in Paris, both hearing and sighted, on December 14, 1880, but the greater part of her childhood was spent in a large family mansion in the city of Tours, in the south of France. Madame Marguerite Pitrois, Yvonne's mother, had been left a widow with two young daughters, Yvonne and an older sister, in Paris, but had initiated a move to Tours, thinking she could more easily raise her daughters there.

Ironically, the expected safe haven became a place of pain, for it was in Tours that Pitrois suffered from sunstroke at the age of seven. After three days of illness, she became deaf, and soon after this, she began to lose her eyesight. Her eyesight intermittently improved and deteriorated, causing deep concern to her and her devoted mother. Her sight was impaired until she was twelve, when she could finally see well enough to read and to write without difficulty.

Without the admirable dedication of her mother, Pitrois might have succumbed more completely to her illnesses. Through her mother's efforts, she also maintained her ability to speak. These trials at an early age developed a high degree of empathy in Yvonne Pitrois. Throughout her life she held a deep concern for deaf, blind, and deaf-blind people, coupled with a determination to give them all the friendship and support that she could.[1]

Pitrois and her mother dealt with her loss of hearing and sight in a variety of unique and creative ways. Pitrois was a precocious child, and she had already learned to read and to write well before the onset of her deafness and blindness. This helped her to endure the years when she had to remain in a dark room for most of the day, and it allowed her mother to tell her stories by writing on the palm of her hand with a finger. In this unusual way, she received instruction in two languages, English and French.

Marguerite Pitrois supported her young daughters by running a school where English people learned French and French people learned English. In time, when Yvonne's blindness was finally cured, she helped her mother with her translation work. This aptitude for languages would later be one of the strengths that would lead Yvonne to her career as a professional writer and translator.

Marguerite Pitrois came to her role as her daughter's teacher quite naturally, through a deep love that was reinforced by her training and professional commitment. Yvonne, during the years of her almost complete blindness, "read stories" that her mother wrote into her hand. Her mother soon began to teach her to lipread. It was a religious household; the family were Huguenots, and the Lord's Prayer provided the first daily lipreading lessons. Yvonne was encouraged to speak by her mother, who was distressed that her daughter, not hearing her own voice any longer, had stopped talking. Throughout her period of convalescence, then, Yvonne was constantly aided by her mother, who offered "refuge and strength" to her daughter.[2]

These were exhausting responsibilities for a woman in frail health herself who was also responsible for the upbringing of another daughter and for providing financial support for the household. In time, the older daughter married a professor and established her own home, and the mother's responsibilities became somewhat lighter. In any case, there was no question in the mother's mind that she would be the educator of her younger daughter. This was perhaps due, in some measure, to Pitrois's blindness, which was total for at least several months after the sunstroke. Her mother earnestly believed that she alone could best give her daughter the personal attention and specialized instruction that she needed.[3]

On the whole, this worked out well, as the mother was well equipped to help her daughter develop her innate gifts of heart and mind. Other deaf children, at this time, were often abandoned and neglected; Pitrois had the good fortune to have a mother who was a devoted and persevering educator. Nor was it an easy task for the mother, for in addition to the skills previously mentioned, she also had to teach her daughter to overcome a timidity that had been made worse by the traumatic experience she had undergone. It was necessary, the mother saw, to encourage her daughter to become more outgoing.

Over the years Pitrois developed into a remarkable woman with kindness and intelligence, according to a critic who was her countryman and her contemporary.[4] She recognized the sacrifices that her mother had made and felt very grateful. She wrote once: "C'est à elle seule que reviennent la peine et l'honneur de mon éducation, je n'ai jamais eu d'autre professeur qu'elle" ("It is to her alone that I owe the effort and honor of my education; she was my only teacher").[5] From the onset of Yvonne's illness, at the age of seven, until she reached the age of sixteen, her mother gave her all of her free time.

On numerous occasions, Yvonne Pitrois spoke of her mother's great patience, particularly during the time of her blindness, and she drew parallels between her mother; Anne Sullivan, who taught Helen Keller; and Sister Sainte Marguerite, who taught Marie Heurtin (a deaf-blind French girl).[6] It is interesting and telling that long after the episode of her blindness, Pitrois still counted herself among deaf-blind people and compared her mother to the most famous teachers of the deaf-blind of her era.

Unlike the teachers of Marie Heurtin and Helen Keller, Marguerite Pitrois had no experience with deaf or deaf-blind people. She managed, nonetheless, to succeed by letting her wisdom and love guide her in mapping out her daughter's education. When questioned about her mother's methodology, Yvonne Pitrois herself recognized this, stating: "Sa seule méthode, c'est son coeur" ("Her only method is her heart").[7] If the mother was extremely devoted, we see that the daughter deeply appreciated it and proved herself worthy of such a mother both in terms of her personal charm and her professional success, for Pitrois had her first book published at the age of eighteen. These early literary triumphs continued, and Pitrois became a prolific and well-respected author.

Pitrois also took great comfort in her Huguenot faith. Although she rarely talked or wrote of it, she revealed this passion for her religion in a short biographical sketch of Bernard Palissy, a celebrated ceramist and convert to Protestantism who lived from 1510 to 1590. His dedication to his art and his faith are both stressed by Pitrois, who portrayed him as a great artist who produced ceramic masterpieces but also left behind the memory of a noble character, strong will, and a conscience without fear and without reproach.[8]

The artist we see in this sketch succeeded at great cost. He suffered great poverty, as did his family, as he sought to devote himself to his art. To the horror of his wife and children, and the contemporary reader, Palissy even sacrificed the tables and chairs in his household to feed the oven's fires as he tried to find the right temperature for his pottery.

Through the influence of Philibert Hamelin, who had arrived from Geneva, Palissy became a Protestant, devoted to purity, austerity, and fraternal love, reflecting the spirit of the Reformation. Although he was originally protected by Catherine de Medici, who recognized his genius, he was finally imprisoned for his beliefs and died of misery and starvation during the reign of Henri III. Pitrois, in the retelling of Bernard's death, railed against Henri III, whom she saw as the most infamous of the kings of France. An accurate historian, she is never dispassionate or aloof; the reader always learns how she feels about her protagonists and their friends and enemies.

Pitrois added that Palissy's artistic genius was now generally recognized in France by artists and by scientists who revered him for his talents. Although she venerated both, she admired his religious strength over his art: "Mais pour nous, enfants de la Réforme, n'est-ce pas encore pour sa fidélité chrétienne et huguenote qu'il est le plus admirable, que nous l'aimons le mieux?" ("But for us, children of the Reformation, isn't it still for his Christian and Huguenot loyalty that he is the most admirable, that we love him the most?").[9] In her own life and literary works, Pitrois was similarly influenced by the moral teachings of her faith, which she manifested in a less extreme way than her hero. Nonetheless, all of her biographies contain a definite sense of austerity and offer serious moral lessons to her readers.

The patient teaching of her mother and the strength that her faith offered her combined to produce a woman with a fine personality. In spite of considerable success, she remained modest and reluctant to talk about herself. She was not worldly or particularly interested in social pleasures. Although she was shy among hearing people when in the larger society, she always had a smile and a lively manner when she was interacting with her friends. She had some initial problems finding her path, however. Did she belong more with hearing people or with deaf people? How could she communicate successfully to be a part of both worlds? These challenging questions were exacerbated by her shyness and the residual memory of her episode with blindness that still filled her with dread.[10]

Pitrois eventually developed a variety of communication techniques. She became a successful lipreader and learned to make herself understood when she spoke. But informal chatting with hearing people who were unaccustomed to communicating with deaf individuals was more challenging for her. She was able to use the manual alphabet and some sign language with the deaf and with the initiated hearing. Further, she had maintained from the time of her blindness the ability to read spelling from her mother's hand, a skill her mother had helped her to develop.

Her major form of communication was through her writing, however, and it was writing that would best help her heal from her fears. Pitrois wrote her first book, *Nobles Vies*, at the age of eighteen. It had three editions, rare for such an early effort. In the course of her career, she wrote more than twenty-five scholarly works, continuing to write until a few years before her death.

The range of Pitrois's work is impressive. She wrote biographies of women and of celebrated American historical figures like Benjamin Franklin and Abraham Lincoln and contributed to many magazines and periodicals, especially magazines of a religious nature or those serving the deaf, and a number of her books and articles were translated into foreign languages. She herself was a fine translator and translated numerous English and American literary works into French. She was able to write almost as fluently in English as in French. Her strong work ethic that led to such an impressive production of work, coupled with her special intellectual gifts, enabled her to earn her living as a writer, not an easy task in any era. She was a perfectionist, never using a typewriter but writing all of her articles in delicate, precise handwriting that was "as clear as print."[11]

All of her writing, throughout her career, revealed her sense of self-sacrifice. She wrote of the need to overcome pride and selfishness and to submit to God's will. This is reflected in her story "Une humble vie ou comment puis-je lui faire du bien?" ("A Humble Life or How Can I Help Him?"). I found this story, published in 1929, in the collections of the Bibliothèque Nationale in Paris. Although it was not specifically aimed at deaf and deaf-blind populations, it summarizes very well the moral convictions of Pitrois.

This short story has two parts. The leading character, Lydie, perhaps more victim than heroine as the story begins, is given an important message by the pastor's wife, Madame Joubert. A hunchback, unattractive, able to walk only with difficulty, Lydie displays, all the same, intelligence and determination. On a visit to Madame Joubert, she confides her secret dream of becoming a missionary. Madame Joubert is forced to confront Lydie with her physical limitations; she says her health would be compromised by such a choice. She advises an alternative path. Why doesn't she bring happiness and consolation to people in her daily life? When she finds herself with a parent, a sibling, a stranger, she must ask herself: "How can I help him or her?"

Lydie is struck by this idea and decides to live by it. She begins by offering flowers to the most hated person in the village, Mother Anselme, and she continues to follow this path by assisting her mother, brothers, and sisters, and many others in the village. Her most dramatic act of goodness is to help her sister Alice, who had lost her way, to find God and salvation before death.

Many of Pitrois's convictions come to the reader through this story.

In Part 2, as an old Lydie looks back on her life, she acknowledges disappointments. But the worst of them, she feels, were not about teasing or ingratitude from other people but arose from times when she had the opportunity to do good for another's benefit and didn't do it, out of a failure of heart or courage.[12] For Pitrois, as for her spokesperson, Lydie, one must live to give support and consolation to others; the major sin is in not giving enough.

In 1912 Pitrois published the work that brought her recognition. It was a biography, the genre in which she would be most successful. In her study of the Abbé de l'Épée, she painted a portrait of a man who increasingly grew into his vocation of helping others, the deaf population, in this case, for the abbé established a government-sponsored school for deaf children in France. His stage was certainly broader than Lydie's, but the elements of self-sacrifice and the powerful desire to serve are strikingly similar.

This biography was published at the time of the bicentenary of the abbé's birth, in time for the World Congress of the Deaf in Paris. She wrote it in celebration of the abbé's memory. She subsequently translated it into English for the *Silent Worker* (an American newspaper published by and for deaf people), which ran the biography serially from October 1912 to January 1913. Her intention was to teach the American deaf population about the life of this benefactor of deaf people.

Pitrois gained fame during the bicentenary, becoming particularly well known in France and America. Her contributions to American periodicals for deaf people became frequent. She entitled her letters to the *Silent Worker* "From the Old World" and educated Americans about deaf people in France, Belgium, and Switzerland. She wrote about European institutions for the deaf and about remarkable European deaf people. She wrote, as well, for the *Volta Review* and the *American Annals of the Deaf*, the leading American deaf education journals for teachers and administrators. She stated her purpose in making these international contributions in her first letter to the *Silent Worker*. It was "to contribute toward extending the bounds of comprehension, sympathy and affection uniting, all the world over, our great silent universal family."[13] She engaged her readers by telling fascinating and moving stories in an accessible manner. Her recounting of the life of the Abbé de l'Épée is no exception; the story is well told, even though it is one of her earlier works and reflects many of the themes and images that typify her biographies.

Pitrois addressed her deaf readers, as she began her tale, exhorting them to learn from the abbé's life and teachings. An interesting tension between light and darkness, and between superficial, glittering wealth and spiritual riches established itself in the narrative early on. Charles-Michel de l'Épée, was born in 1712 in Versailles, the city that had served as the residence to the king of France and to his whole court. The carriages covered with paintings and gold, and the elegant ladies transported in them, were among the early memories of the abbé.

His own family had comfortable wealth; his father was an architect for the king. Although this father was a good Christian and gave a good moral education to his children, he was not eager for his son to enter the priesthood. But the future abbé had been intrigued by Jansenism and felt unable to sign a necessary declaration condemning it as he terminated his studies. Alienated from his vocation for a number of years, then, the abbé was only marginally a priest. Although he had the habit and the title of priest, he was unable to perform his professional functions. Ironically, it is through his encounter with deaf twins, socially marginal themselves, that the abbé would again find his role as a priest and his place on the world scene.

In 1760, the abbé went to Fossés Saint-Victor Street in Paris on business. He stumbled into an unknown house and came upon a room in which two fifteen-year-old young women were sewing. They were simply clothed in long dark wool dresses. Concerned that he might have frightened them, the abbé explained that he had lost his way, but strangely, the girls didn't answer and, in fact, showed no emotion; their faces were plunged in darkness, a darkness that, we'll see later, reflects their inability to communicate and their spiritual isolation:

"Les deux adolescentes ne répondirent pas un mot; pas un reflet d'é-motion, de reconnaissance, n'éclaira leur visage terne, ne fit briller leurs regards toujours fixés sur l'inconnu avec un morne étonnement" ("The two adolescents didn't say a word; no trace of emotion or gratitude lit up their dark faces or made their eyes, still fixed on the unknown man with a somber astonishment, shine").[14]

As the abbé, perplexed and hurt by the girls' refusal to speak to him, gets ready to depart, the mother arrives and explains that her daughters are deaf. The abbé is surprised; this was the first time that he had seen deaf people. This was none too rare, Pitrois intervenes in her narrative and tells us, as, in the eighteenth century, it was still considered an embarrassment to have deaf people in one's family; they were often hidden, abandoned on the streets, or relegated to the darkest corners of their homes.

In spite of relative poverty and limited education, the mother recognized that her daughters had loving hearts and intelligence. Unlike many of her contemporaries, she cherished her daughters and sought and found a teacher for them to prepare them for their First Communion. But now, she told the abbé, Father Vanin had died, and she feared isolation and rejection for her daughters: "Mes filles sont retombées dans la nuit de l'ignorance, de l'inconscience" ("My daughters have fallen back into the night of ignorance and unawareness").[15]

The abbé, saddened by the mother's story and eager to free the girls from their prison of silence and lead them to God, assumed the task of educating the twins, to the relief and delight of their mother. In a house he shared with his brother in Paris, 14 rue des Moulins, the abbé received the two deaf girls. Already past fifty, he wondered whether he could succeed at this task that was so new and difficult for him. Pitrois's imagery gives us a foreshadowing of the abbé's future success. Researching the work of those who had preceded him, studying signs and the manual alphabet, the abbé, above all, sought insight through prayer and "demande à Dieu ses lumières" ("asks God to illuminate his path").[16] The reader senses that these lights will replace the darkness that had enveloped the lives of the twin sisters, in spite of their mother's best efforts. To help the twin sisters find salvation, the abbé fully embraced his vocation through his work with them. To teach his students not only secular subjects but the mysteries of his Christian faith, the abbé released his affinity for Jansenism and fully submitted to his church.

Soon the abbé became totally consumed by the work, transforming rooms of his house into a school, the first that existed for deaf children. By 1785, twenty-five years after the opening of the school, there were seventy-two students. The abbé managed to find places to lodge the boys and girls, overcoming societal prejudices and paying the expenses of the poor himself. His life belonged to deaf people, the abbé would say, no matter what their social class or country of origin.[17]

He was seen as a pioneer who helped to shape the children's minds and souls. Isolated in society, the children became a family at the school and had, in him, a person totally devoted to their needs. After a few years, the abbé gave back to their parents young people who were educated socially and religiously, able to earn their own living and "de tenir dignement leur place au soleil" ("to have their place in the sun").[18] Their education had moved them from dark hiding places in their parents' homes into daylight and their rightful place in society.

The abbé's horizons expanded, as did the children's. To serve the deaf communities in other countries, he studied Italian, Spanish, German, and English. He had public "séances" or classes to demonstrate his work, although it went against his spirit of humility, believing that he had to demonstrate the potential of deaf people to the attention of the public. He became politically involved in the "Solar Affair." Certain that an abandoned young deaf boy was Joseph, the orphan of the Count of Solar, the abbé fought, albeit unsuccessfully, for his rights. It was a first effort to bring justice to deaf people, nonetheless. (See pp. 56–58 for further explanation of this incident.)

And with this increased visibility came fame. The abbé's school received noteworthy visitors, among them the Emperor of Austria, Joseph II, and Catherine II of Russia. And soon the abbé had many disciples, too. Among the most famous of these was the Abbé Sicard, who, along with Saint-Sernin founded the future National Institution of the Deaf in Bordeaux.

Later in life, in 1774, a new frontier came to mind for the abbé, a wish to support and to teach every deaf-blind student anywhere in the world:

> J'offre de tout mon coeur à ma patrie et aux nations voisines de me charger de l'instruction d'un enfant—s'il s'en trouve—qui étant sourd et muet, serait devenu aveugle à l'âge de deux ou trois ans. Plût à la miséricorde divine qu'il n'y ait jamais une personne sur la terre qui soit éprouvée d'une manière aussi terrible! Mais s'il en est une seule, je souhaite qu'on me l'amène, et de pouvoir contribuer par mes soins au grand ouvrage de son salut. (I make the offer with all my heart to my country and to neighboring nations to take charge of the instruction of a child—if such exists—who being deaf and dumb, might have become blind at the age of two or three. Please Divine Providence that there may never be a person on this earth who is tested in as terrible a manner! But if there is a single one, I wish for him to be brought to me, and to be able to contribute by my care to the great work of his salvation.)[19]

In spite of this touching appeal, the abbé never discovered the desired deaf-blind student. He had conducted active research throughout Europe during the last years of his life but these children, Pitrois sadly tells us, were well hidden, for families were more ashamed of them than of their deaf children. Perhaps, Pitrois continued to ruminate, God felt the abbé had done enough and wanted to leave to another the supreme task of making him known and loved by deaf-blind people.

Pitrois concludes this biography with a moral lesson to her deaf-blind sisters and brothers. She tells them that the miracles they realized in their education are due to the abbé's early efforts, the methods that he developed, and his drive to help the disabled. Pitrois asks her deaf-blind friends to join deaf people in thanking the abbé, the first who wanted to bring a ray of light into their night.

In Pitrois's first serious biographical effort she has begun to explore a favorite audience, that of the deaf-blind community, whom she will focus on in her research and writing, and try to help in other ways. She will speak of blind and deaf-blind, their parents and teachers, the men and women who lightened their burden or failed to do so. She will use images of light and shadows to emphasize and symbolize the themes of her various works and, in so doing, she will also find a way to free herself of the haunting memory of her own episode of deaf-blindness.

Her participation in L'Epée's bicentenary appears to have given direction to her career. In an interesting duplication of her hero's trajectory, Pitrois found, in writing about the abbé's discovery of the deaf sisters and his ensuing commitment to that population, her own strong connection to that community and her desire to serve it. The one significant deprivation she suffered in being educated by her mother alone was the lack of exposure to the society of other deaf people.

By 1912 Pitrois and her mother had left their large house in Tours, to move to Le Mans in the province of Sarthé. Pitrois had the idea of publishing a letter in the magazine of the Y.W.C.A. in order to express her concern for deaf individuals. Soon another reader wrote to her of a lonely deaf girl in the country and suggested that Pitrois write to her. Pitrois eagerly wrote this first letter. Soon she would find a more structured way to establish linkages with many other deaf correspondents, something she had long wanted to do.

As a young person, Pitrois had written to the famous deaf poet, Helen Marion Burnside, expressing her desire to establish a correspondence club for the deaf people of the Western world. But the busy Englishwoman told her that she had no time to do this. In 1912, some sixteen years later, the same idea occurred to Mrs. James Muir, a deaf woman from Australia, and a Cosmopolitan Correspondence Club was established. Through Muir's correspondence club, Pitrois became acquainted with Helen Keller, the American deaf sculptor Douglas Tilden, and the French deaf-blind poet Bertha Galeron de Calonne, as well as with François Coppée, Alphonse Daudet, Pierre Loti and other French men of letters.

On Christmas Eve of 1912, Pitrois launched *La Petite Silencieuse*, a more sophisticated way of corresponding with other deaf women than she had found thus far. She was able to do this because she had, at this time, both more leisure and more financial security. Her hope was to offer direct help through this periodical. It was printed at her expense, issued bimonthly, and had about fourteen pages, selling at twenty cents a copy.

The charming magazine with its blue cover circulated throughout France, Switzerland, and Canada. There was a tone of intimacy, and Pitrois's concern for her readers and affection for them was apparent. There were soon some nine hundred "little sisters" who were subscribing. Pitrois wrote to almost all of them personally and knew them as individuals. The magazine was part newspaper, part literary journal, part counsel through letters. Each issue had an inspiring editorial, written by Pitrois herself, news of interest to the deaf community, and letters on a variety of subjects from the subscribers, filled with human interest: moving and amusing, in turn. The subscribers might recount the illness or death of a parent, the birth of a child, fears for a harvest, or announcements of meetings with former classmates and teachers.

Their stories, as heartwarming as they were, were dwarfed by the power of the tales Pitrois told in her editorials. Often she recounted humble lives made beautiful by a person's spirit of sacrifice. One of the most touching of these is her story of the life and secret of Marie-Jeanne Meunier, in a 1913 issue of *La Petite Silencieuse*. The story bears the title "Une humble Chrétienne" ("A Humble Christian").[20]

Marie-Jeanne Meunier, who lived from 1806 to 1877, had been abandoned as a baby. She was sent to an asylum for orphans but was later accepted at the deaf institute in Paris as an act of charity. Although her intellectual gifts were somewhat limited, she was earnest in her studies, and she became an excellent seamstress and a patient teacher of these skills to the young women. (This was, Pitrois the careful historian tells us, during the time of the Abbé Sicard.) She had a good heart and also tried her best to help one of the deaf-blind students at the Paris Institute at that time, Octavie Morisseau. The latter had been deaf and became blind later on, and Marie-Jeanne offered herself to the girl as guide, interpreter, and adviser.

But a mystery surfaced concerning what appeared to be miserliness on the part of Meunier, a seemingly noble woman. She would go on no trips, nor would she go out with the other young women to buy pretty clothing, or even sit with them and share a lunch or dinner in a café outside the walls of the institute. She bought little for herself or for colleagues. This behavior was much frowned upon, and she was privately criticized for it.

The mystery was solved only upon her death. When her last wishes were read, it was seen that out of her small wages, she had saved several thousand francs. And she had left all of these savings to the National Institute to help some future students, penniless and possibly orphaned, as she had been, to attend the school.

Pitrois's awareness of the life of Octavie Morisseau, which provides a story within a story in her tale of Marie-Jeanne, reminds us again of her desire to serve deaf-blind people as well as the deaf and hard-of-hearing populations. Early on, she had written to Helen Keller, encouraging her to publish a magazine for Americans who were deaf-blind. But when this didn't materialize, Pitrois took on the mission for herself.

For several years after having launched *La Petite Silencieuse*, Pitrois dedicated one page of it to messages to and from deaf-blind readers. Finally, in 1928, Pitrois published a magazine specifically for deaf-blind readers. It was most probably the first magazine ever devoted to this population. It was published in French Braille and appeared every three months. She called her magazine *Le Rayon de Soleil des Sourds-Aveugles* (*The Sunbeam of the Deaf-Blind*). In it, she shared her own personal stories and experiences with her readers, but the greater part of the magazine focused on an exchange of thoughts, ideas, and gifts among the deaf-blind readers. In friendship and compassion, they sent one another presents that would bring solace and joy. One deaf-blind peasant girl in a distant village in the Alps sent Pitrois a pair of stockings she had knitted and asked her "dear big sister" to forward it to an even lonelier deaf-blind girl. Others knit gloves, made pearl necklaces and chains, dressed rag dolls, and sent them to her to be distributed to unknown friends. Many did without necessities in order to send gifts to others whom they believed were more in need.*

Through her magazine Pitrois established a circle of friendship among her subscribers and encouraged them to perform exercises in charity. And Pitrois, herself, participated in this exercise in generosity. In addition to facilitating this exchange of gifts, she obtained literature in Braille for her readers and organized a fund to give small sums of money, at certain times of the year, to the deaf-blind sisters most in need in order to improve their lives. Pitrois's *Le Rayon de Soleil* had more than one hundred readers in France, Canada, and the United States, ranging in age from ten to eighty-five. The magazine was sent free of charge to them all.

A contemporary critic observed that the deaf and deaf-blind readers reciprocated Pitrois's affection for them and they appreciated her efforts on their behalf. All gave loving accounts of their "big sister" and of her timely intervention in their lives.[21] They spoke of how she had extended herself to bring friends, help, and jobs when they most needed such support and were unable to find it anywhere else.

Pitrois's dedication to the deaf-blind population continued throughout her life and was reflected in the biographies and other works that she wrote. In addition to her publication of *Le Rayon de Soleil*, she wrote a study of the Heurtin family in *Volta Review* in 1911; an analysis of Helen Keller in 1922, in *Une nuit rayonnante: Helen Keller*, a portrait of "A Deaf-Blind Hero of France"; in 1925 in *The Silent Worker*, *Sourds-Muets-Aveugles* (*Deaf-Blind*), a lengthy work published in 1929; and *Trois Lumières dans la Nuit: Valentin Haüy, Louis Braille, Maurice de la Sizeranne* (*Three Lights in the Darkness: Valentin Haüy, Louis Braille, Maurice de la Sizeranne*) (1936), possibly her most highly developed work in this area of her literary output. All of these works focus on those who worked to liberate the deaf-blind, as well as deaf-blind people themselves, who were less and less portrayed as victims in her work.

---

*In his history on Pitrois, Lang underlines on page 293 of *Deaf Persons in the Arts and Sciences* the moving generosity of Pitrois's readers.

While eager to tell the stories of ordinary people, Pitrois also wanted to recount the lives and triumphs of the more famous deaf and deaf-blind men and women of her age. Unfortunately, she never told her own story in full, but because of her own delight in reading, research, and study, she had a unique ability to understand and portray the literary mind, and her biography of Helen Keller is among the best of her works.

Both Keller and Pitrois were gifted writers, knew of one another, and corresponded with one another. Both were impressively bilingual in English and French. Helen Keller had written a letter to Pitrois in 1913, intended for publication in *La Petite Silencieuse*. Pitrois posted it in the page providing news to the deaf-blind readers, in particular. In it, Keller spoke of being on the lecture circuit with her teacher, Anne Sullivan: "J'essaie d'apporter un message de lumière à ceux sur lesquels est tombée la nuit de la cécité, physique ou spirituelle" ("I am trying to bring a message of light to those on whom the physical or spiritual night of blindness has fallen").[22] This was a goal that Pitrois definitely shared.

It was predictable, then, that Pitrois would want to do a study of her friend and contemporary. Pitrois traced well the early development of Helen, born hearing and sighted into a wealthy family in Tuscumbia, Alabama. A precocious child, she had spoken her first words at the age of six months. Before reaching the age of two, however, she had been rendered deaf and blind as the result of a childhood illness. And Pitrois, remembering well her own episode of blindness, speaks of Helen's imprisonment in this "double night" of deafness and blindness.

It was Anne Sullivan, sent to the Keller family by the Perkins Institution, who would bring Helen back from the chaos into which her life had fallen. Through Anne's efforts and skill, Helen reacquired language and thought. And Pitrois tells well the familiar tale of Anne's pumping water on one of Helen's hands, while spelling "water" into the other hand. It was a word that Helen had retained from her early childhood, and it broke through the wall of isolation. From these small beginnings would come a life of impressive intellectual achievements, among them Keller's graduation from Radcliffe College at age twenty-four, with a bachelor of arts degree and with honors in English.

What is unique in Pitrois's biography of Keller, however, is her emphasis on Keller's moral development. Believing that Keller's intelligence and strength of will were justifiably celebrated, Pitrois felt that Keller's character was less well known. She had, according to Pitrois, a charming tenderness and goodness of heart. As early as the first Christmas in which she had reacquired language, Helen showed a profound generosity. She offered a goblet, a treasured gift she had received, to a poor child in Tuscumbia who was standing near the Christmas tree in sadness because he had received no gifts.

These early tendencies only grew through the years. Although Pitrois found Helen Keller's early religious education lacking, she credited her with eventually developing a strong belief in God and the brotherhood of man. These principles, Pitrois told the reader, led Keller to a personal courage and a continuing desire to encourage others. Another aspect of Pitrois's literary representation of the deaf and the deaf-blind experience was reflected in her activities during the Great War, World War I. Pitrois and her family had moved from Tours to Bordeaux before the outbreak of the war. Soon Marguerite Pitrois began to support the war effort by volunteering as a trained nurse, until her health dictated a complete rest. Yvonne took as her personal mission to support deaf and deaf-blind people during this period of upheaval and trauma. She helped many deaf people with life's necessities. She helped to find aid to support deaf refugees and their families, to place deaf children in school programs and to find deaf adults employment. She also brought necessary attention to their plight by reporting on their situation in *The Silent Worker*. In 1914 and 1915, she wrote many articles discussing the dire plight of the French and Belgian deaf and gathered money to help them, often from American readers. These impressive efforts were recognized after the war. She was decorated by the King of Belgium, and in 1920, she received a Medal of Honor from the French Welfare Society "for devotion to mankind."[23] Her literary work was similarly recognized by the French government and she was made an officer of the French Academy.

All of the honors were well deserved. In 1918 Pitrois wrote a letter to encourage and thank all soldiers who were fighting and dying for France. In "Lettre d'une Française à Nos Soldats" ("Letter from a Frenchwoman to Our Soldiers"), Pitrois's patriotism and religiosity come together as she urges the soldiers to fight to keep France alive. As she said, they must live in the new France that will emerge, but if they must die, they will be received by God, who will gather to him all those who fought and suffered for such a saintly cause.[24]

But she well understood the price that heroism often exacted from the soldiers, as demonstrated in her portrait of Paul Houpert, "A Deaf-Blind Hero of France," written for *The Silent Worker*, in 1925.[25] Long after the war's end, Houpert was still struggling with the physical and emotional impact of his war experiences. A humble man, born into a poor family, Houpert's story is poignant in its depiction of a man who accepts his fate and constantly sacrifices his own comfort and welfare for the benefit of others. To the modern reader, there is an unavoidable sense of wasted potential, for he had literary and intellectual gifts that were lost through the dire circumstances he had to deal with. Pitrois did not share this assessment. For her, the development of Houpert's character would trump such concerns.

At the beginning of her story Pitrois observed that although Paul was blind and nearly deaf and the right side of his body almost paralyzed as a result of wounds received during the Great War, he had managed to write a thirty-two-page manuscript telling his story. Pitrois's only work was to abridge it and translate it into English.

It was a story of personal sacrifice even before Paul entered the military. To help his Alsatian parents, who had nine other children, he gave up his love of study to work as a glassmaker like his older brother, completing his apprenticeship at the age of sixteen. A few pleasures, like his participation in a music society, brightened his life. In 1914, he enlisted in the army to fight in the Great War. Volunteering to serve in the trenches, he was sent to Verdun, where he received twenty-one wounds and, at one point, was close to death. He was saved by a Red Cross worker who took him off the field and brought him to a hospital.

Knowing he was deaf and partially crippled, Paul at first thought he still had vision in one eye. In a misguided effort to keep him calm or protect him, the doctors had deceived him. He felt great heartache when he discovered that he was both deaf and blind, he tells the reader. But in one of many heroic moments, Paul decided to accept his fate. And in his many hospital stays, it was he who encouraged the other soldiers, although he was usually the most seriously wounded.

Bravely attempting to reconstruct his life, Paul learned new trades at the military school in Reuilly: brushmaking, shoemaking, basketwork, thread-making, with machine knitting being his favorite trade and reading still his favorite source of pleasure. To that end, he studied abbreviated Braille, teaching himself to read. He met and married the maid of one of the nurses in 1919, a sweet girl who brought happiness into his life. In 1921, Paul and his wife had, to his delight, a son also named Paul. But his life remained difficult; he was dogged by poverty and illness but insisted in the conclusion to his short biography that he found life well worth living.

Pitrois added some comments to his conclusion. She spoke of his beautiful character, his fortitude, his optimism, and his ability to triumph over his afflictions. Far from being overwhelmed by the enormity of his suffering, she focused on small ways in which his life could be made more enjoyable. She had already begun a correspondence with him, becoming an adopted "godmother" to Houpert. And now she offered his address to readers of *The Silent Worker*, asking for correspondents who were able to write in Braille. He was eager to hear from deaf or deaf-blind American soldiers, Pitrois stated.

Pitrois was dedicated to deaf, blind, and deaf-blind individuals, but she was equally dedicated to the schools, institutions, and homes that provided them with shelter, nurturing, and education. Pitrois collected postcards with images of these organizations and had a personal library of books by and about deaf people; she particularly enjoyed books that discussed the historical origins of deaf institutions. Like Berthier, she believed that all deaf children should be taught deaf history: "As the American children are taught the history of America and the French children the history of France, so the deaf children of all nations must be taught the History of the Deaf and their Friends."[26]

In her articles for *The Silent Worker* and *The Volta Review* she provided a complete discussion of the philanthropic activity in Europe that led to the development of institutions, schools, and associations for the deaf. In such endeavors, she explained how the efforts of the poor and resources of the rich could come together to further the cause of the deaf community. She wrote often, as well, about how a kind priest, teacher, or philanthropist had initiated such efforts on behalf of deaf people.

Basing her article in part on information provided her by her friend and writing colleague Corinne Rocheleau, whom she saw as one of the cleverest of the former students of the Montreal Institute for Deaf Girls, Pitrois traced the history of this French school for deaf girls that began through the founding of the Sisterhood of Providence by Madame Yamelin.[27] Her husband and three children had died, so she took as family the neglected and poor on this earth.

At the time that Madame Yamelin founded the sisterhood, a wealthy and respected family named Gadbois lived near Montreal. The father and mother had eight children, one son and seven daughters. The son died young, and subsequently, all seven daughters chose to become nuns. Five of the seven daughters entered the religious order founded by Madame Yamelin.

One of the young sisters, Aline Gadbois, or Sister Marie de Bon Secours, was working among the mentally ill in 1850, one of the populations cared for by the Sisters of Providence at that time. She noticed that a few deaf girls were forced to live among the mentally ill because they were unable to hear or speak. Her heart was moved by this difficult situation; she had particular pity for a bright little girl, Marguerite Hanley. Sister Marie felt something needed to be done for these imprisoned souls. But what? She met a priest, the Abbé Lagorce, who had just begun to teach deaf boys and was about to open the school for French Catholic deaf boys in Montreal. The abbé gave Sister Marie some counsel and lessons about teaching "the silent."

Marguerite Hanley, Sister Marie's first student, made good progress, and Mother Yamelin and the Bishop of Montreal became interested in her work. Soon the project for the Catholic Institute for French Canadian Deaf Girls developed. Sister Marie became the founder and the first head of the new school. Three of her sisters followed her as head of the school that originally used the combined method (the use of signs and speech to communicate with deaf children).

The Gadbois sisters ran the institute for fifty-five years. Their direction was firm and wise and the institute flourished. In their commitment, they devoted both their lives and their parents' fortune to it. They were highly educated, fluent in English and French, and knowledgeable in both law and mathematics, and they were completely dedicated to the children they taught and worked with.

At the time that Pitrois wrote her article, there had been fifteen Mothers Superior, including the Gadbois sisters; the current director was Sister Alphonse du Sauveur. The institution was important not only to the deaf population in the community, but also to those who were deaf and blind. Pitrois reminded readers of Corinne Rouleau's work about Ludivine Lachance, *Out of Her Prison . . .*, which had been honored by the French Academy and which she saw as a beautiful book (see chap. 5 for further explanation of this work). Ludivine, the wild deaf-blind heroine who, through the intervention of the nuns at the Mon-treal Institute, became gentle and achieved sainthood, had died of consumption some years earlier. But Sister Angélique-Marie, who had taught her, now had in her care eight adult deaf-blind residents in the convent. An aged nun who had lost her hearing and later her vision joined the others. A large room in the Salle Bonsecours was set aside for them, in addition to a workroom. They had Braille books and desks and typewriters. They sewed, knitted, made bags and baskets, and wove. In June of 1933 their work was exhibited at the Montreal Exhibition, where it received the highest awards and was greatly admired. Pitrois expressed her admiration for this amazing work on the part of the sisters and the several founders of this remarkable institution that served the deaf and the deaf-blind students equally well.

Another institution highly regarded by Pitrois was Notre-Dame de Larnay, near Poitiers. Her fascination with this school and the population it served stemmed from her interest in the Heurtin family. As early as March of 1911, Pitrois wrote a sketch of this family of nine children of a Breton cooper and his cousin. Four of the children died young, and of the remaining five, only two were born without disabilities.[28]

In her early study of the family, Pitrois discussed in some detail the efforts undertaken on behalf of the son, Stanislas, who was deaf and almost blind, at the Persagotière, a school for deaf and deaf-blind boys in Nantes, run by the Brothers of Saint-Gabriel. The boys were given good vocational training through the oral method, learning to be shoemakers, tailors, gardeners, joiners, turners, and printers. Although he had come to the school at eight, very undisciplined, Stanislas soon won people's hearts through his good character and kind disposition. In a process that became familiar to her readers, Pitrois and her mother went to visit Stanislas and the deaf school for boys as Pitrois was researching her article. They found him less interesting than his deaf-blind sisters, but still charming.

It was the deaf-blind Heurtin sisters, educated at Larnay, who particularly fascinated Yvonne Pitrois. She analyzed their development in depth in her work *Sourds-Muets-Aveugles!*[29] The work provides a brief history of some early relative successes in the education of deaf-blind individuals around the world, but it is Part 3 of the study, outlining the work at Larnay, that is of the greatest interest. Under the guidance of the Sisters of Wisdom, more than three hundred deaf inhabitants of all ages lived and learned together. The youngest were taught to read and to speak.

The first deaf-blind person to be educated at Larnay was Marthe Obrecht. She was an Alsatian child who lost her hearing and sight through fright during the Franco-Prussian War (1870–1871) after her town had been bombarded. She had been put on a train like a package and sent to the sisters without any advance notice. She was an inert mass when the sisters received her, but they succeeded in teaching her to read, to write in Braille, to express herself through signs and to work manually, all the same. She later developed a spiritual connection to God and religion.

The most impressive period at Larnay, however, began on March 1, 1895, with the arrival of the wild, screaming Marie Heurtin. Marie was ten and had been deaf-blind from birth. She fought against her desperate condition, her silence and darkness, so furiously that she was thought to be insane, as well. Her response to her profound disability differed dramatically from that of her predecessor, but both showed extreme distress in their sense of alienation from the people around them.

Marie was soon taken under the wing of Sister Sainte Marguerite, who had trained in working with deaf-blind people and had a natural aptitude for it. After a few months, Sister Sainte Marguerite broke through the communication barrier and succeeded in teaching Marie the word "knife." Marie had a small pocketknife that she liked, and this became the basis for the first lessons. Sister Marguerite would take it from her and give it back to her when she made the correct sign for it. It was her first word and her first thought, a key word like Helen Keller's "water." It was soon followed by a second word and sign, "egg," as she liked this food.

The more language she learned, the more control she gained over her anger. She became a child like any other, soon surpassing others in her spirituality. While her brilliant sister in misfortune, Helen Keller, had attained the summits of intellectual life, she attained in her peaceful study the summits of mystical life.

In 1902 another deaf-blind girl was born to the Heurtin family. But the family now had hope for such a child, having witnessed the remarkable development of Marie, and Marthe Heurtin was helped more by her family and those living near her childhood home. Her family planned for her to join her older sister at Larnay, where Sister Marguerite would teach her, too. But in 1910, terrible news spread throughout the deaf and deaf-blind community. Sister Marguerite, the devoted educator of Marie Heurtin and others, had been taken in a matter of days by pneumonia. It fell to Sister Saint Louis to continue her work, with the aid of Marie Heurtin, who was now skilled enough to become a second teacher to her sister. Pitrois, who had visited Larnay, wrote of seeing the two sisters bent over their task together, Marie, as frail as a lily, and her young, sturdier sister, as fresh as a rose. Marie would guide her sister's hesitant fingers over the raised letters of the books.

With an ethereal demeanor that seemed to be not completely of this world, Marie died in 1921 at the age of thirty-six, of a seemingly mild illness that turned serious. Pitrois tells us that "elle s'endormit dans les ténèbres qui, pour elle, avaient toujours couvert la terre pour se réveiller aux radieuses clartés du ciel, dans les bras de sa bien-aimée Soeur Sainte Marguerite et sûrement de là-Haut, elle a continué à protéger de façon plus efficace encore la petite soeur qu'elle chérissait" ("she fell asleep in the shadows that, for her, had always covered the earth to awaken in the radiant light of the sky, in the arms of her beloved Sister Sainte Marguerite and assuredly from above, she continued to protect in an even more successful manner the little sister she cherished").[30]

At the time of this later work on the Heurtin family, the little sister, Marthe, was twenty-seven and, according to Pitrois, was gracious, charming, and accomplished. She had learned to accept her disability not only with peace but with joy, feeling that it united her with Jesus. She had the companionship of others, as there were now ten deaf-blind girls at Larnay's school, which continued to educate them, occupy them, and provide them with a home.

Pitrois, applauding this work, makes a touching appeal to her readers, urging them to reach out to deaf-blind people, to cross the divide between themselves and this population. Deaf-blind people may appear impassive, but there is a need to go beneath the surface in order to communicate with them and open their souls. There are now many ways to communicate with deaf-blind people—through the manual alphabet of the Abbé de l'Épée, through sign language, through the tactile alphabet, or through writing with the finger on the hand of the other person, the method that Pitrois's mother had used with her. Again, in her wisdom, Pitrois found simple ways for all of us to improve the spiritual life of even the most disabled people among us.

All of Pitrois's subjects either have or develop a strong character, and they stop being victims once they are offered an opportunity to live life with some dignity. In her book *Trois lumières dans la nuit: Valentin Haüy, Louis Braille, Maurice de la Sizeranne* (*Three Lights in the Darkness . . .*), the three heroes, although disabled themselves, far from being victims, are presented as excellent role models for the blind, deaf, and deaf-blind communities for whom Pitrois wrote. All three changed the situation of the blind dramatically—Haüy and Braille by improving their system of education, and de la Sizeranne by helping them socially and materially. All three made these contributions in spite of their own disabilities. Of the three, Haüy alone was not blind, but he became deaf in later years.

Valentin Haüy (1745–1822), a sighted man, was drawn to his vocation in 1771, at the age of twenty-six. Walking through the streets of Paris, he saw ten blind men being exhibited at a street fair. They were grotesquely dressed, with long robes, pointed hats, and fake eyeglasses and were being mocked by spectators. Haüy was horrified by the cruelty of this spectacle, and resolved to make it possible for the blind to become educated. He kept his word, developing a system of raised letters, a precursor of Braille, and spent his life teaching blind children, a life not without other challenges. Forced to flee France for Germany and Russia after the French Revolution, he was allowed to return to see the school for the blind he had helped to develop in 1821, just a year before his death.

Louis Braille (1809–1852) was an adolescent at the Institute for the Blind when Haüy made his last visits there. A brilliant young blind person with a great thirst for knowledge, Braille was frustrated by the cumbersome nature of the early method invented by Haüy. He knew that it could be improved. In 1825, at the age of sixteen, he developed a system of raised dots by which all letters and numbers could be represented. Although the system was enthusiastically received by students and teachers, it was not officially sanctioned by the directors of the institute until twenty-five years later.

Although distressed by this mystifying resistance and plagued by frail health, Braille graciously stayed on at the institution, becoming one of its most effective and generous instructors. Like Haüy, he lived to see his work widely accepted. Several days before his death, he heard the announcement at an official assembly at the school that the merits of his Braille alphabet were undeniable and that in the future all books would be made available in this format.

Educational opportunities for blind people were now much improved, but it remained essential for someone to help them find their place in society. This became the task of Maurice de la Sizeranne (1857–1924). The only one of the three born into a wealthy family, de la Sizeranne was blinded at nine as a result of a childhood game with a bow and arrow. He demonstrated a remarkable sensitivity to his blind brothers who were less privileged. Starting modestly, by helping a few blind friends find jobs, he established, in time, an impressive network of social services that would support blind people from birth to death. As Haüy had been challenged by political events and Braille by administrative resistance, de la Sizeranne finally became exhausted from the impact of World War I, which resulted in the addition of three thousand blind soldiers to his "Association Valentin Haüy pour le bien des aveugles" (Valentin Haüy Association to Promote the Welfare of the Blind). He retired in 1918 and died six years later.

Each portrait is distinct from the other, but they are structurally linked in interesting ways by Pitrois. She shows the reader three heroes who overcame great odds, including the temptation to become bitter. In a personal conclusion to her work, Pitrois departs from her role as objective biographer to add some personal observations. While acknowledging that few of us have the talent and the moral resources of these men, she exhorts us to bring a single light into the nights of evil and suffering. Every good deed, she assures us, is multiplied in time.

As she fortified her readers with tales of heroic lives, Pitrois fortified herself, as well, in recounting such lives. Triumphing over her own fears, she faced the difficulties of her own life with much grace. Perhaps no single event was as challenging for her as the death of her mother on December 2, 1926. Pitrois wrote to her "little sisters" in *La*

Petite Silencieuse only four days later, partly to keep her commitment to her readers, but also demonstrating her professionalism.[31] The newspaper served as an avenue both for self-expression and for connection, and as Pitrois wrote of the loss of her mother, she gave voice to her pain, perhaps bringing it under control, at least to some degree. And the "little sisters" who read the newspaper clearly shared her sorrow, reminding Pitrois that she was not alone in her grief.

In this essay, one of Pitrois's most touching and personal ones, she describes the courageous manner in which her mother faced death. God took her, according to Pitrois, after a long and painful illness that lasted more than a year. Her mother suffered so greatly that Pitrois tried not to think about it. The last two months, her mother's very last days with their nights filled with anguish, were particularly terrible, Pitrois tells her little sisters.

But her mother suffered with great Christian courage, showing an acceptance of God's will. At the end, barely conscious and no longer recognizing her daughters, who were crying at her bedside, she continued to pray, lifting her hands toward God and finally finding release from suffering in her last minutes.

Pitrois sadly describes what she lost in losing her mother. They had been constant companions and had lived in perfect harmony, without any cloud obscuring their tenderness for one another: "Ce que l'un disait, l'autre le pensait. Nous n'étions qu'un coeur et qu'une âme" ("What one said, the other was thinking. We were just one heart and one soul").[32]

Their closeness arose from Pitrois's childhood misfortune, which her mother had responded to with tenacity and creativity. Her early childhood had been spent listening to her mother's songs, which reminded little Yvonne of the songs of birds. But Pitrois tells us that after three days of illness, a sunstroke had rendered her completely deaf and partially deprived of speech at the age of seven. Her mother's songs would remain only in the realm of her memory. Oddly enough, in this fairly complete account of her illness, one of only a few that she gives, she is silent on the almost total blindness that she also suffered for five years.

Had she adjusted to this painful memory? Or was it still too difficult to write about?

Already in these early years, her mother had fragile health, Pitrois sadly stated. In spite of this, she accomplished a great deal. She created a home for her family and particularly enjoyed decorating it. She was a professional teacher, and for many years, she taught foreign students from the best families, until she finally retired and took a well-deserved rest. But writing was her great passion, and when Pitrois's education was almost complete, she returned to literature. She was particularly happy to see Pitrois following in her footsteps and becoming a writer.

Her mother especially enjoyed writing books for children, and she kept up a correspondence with the children she wrote for in periodicals designed for children, *La Fourmi* (*The Ant*) and the *Lectures Illustrées* (*Illustrated Readings*). She called herself the "Bonne Amie" (Good Friend) of the children, counseling them, encouraging them, and help-ing them build good character. She wanted, in fact, to turn all of the children's souls toward God. Her advice was so wise that adults often stepped in and participated in the discussions that Marguerite Pitrois had with her young readers. She was beloved in religious settings, too, as she told stories with strong moral lessons for people of all ages.

She accomplished a lot through the strength of her character, as well as through her writing. In spite of the cruel disappointments in her life, she was an example of courage and happiness. Through her innate gift of empathy, she could offer the afflicted exactly the words they needed to hear, sometimes changing the lives of those to whom she wrote.

Her advice was offered to the humblest and highest placed in society alike. A poor workman, hearing of the death of Marguerite Pitrois, wrote to Yvonne and told her that her mother had offered encourage-ment to his aunt Pauline when she was ready to surrender to despair. Her existence took a different and a better path after Marguerite's wise and patient counseling. At the other end of the spectrum, a woman highly placed in society, the widow of a general, wrote of her sorrow at the death of Marguerite Pitrois. She had greatly admired her and thought of her courage when she fell into sadness. She was sure that

Pitrois would keep the memory of her mother alive. Yvonne Pitrois also took particular note of her mother's support of and connection to her work with deaf and deaf-blind people. Marguerite Pitrois was devoted to the little deaf girls for whom Yvonne wrote her newsletter. She not only encouraged Yvonne to do the work, knowing it brought her consolation and joy, but she was always ready to receive those who came to visit and answer letters written to her. For many years, she helped Pitrois's little deaf-blind protégée, Marthe Heurtin. She visited Larnay with Yvonne and offered wise counsel through letters and in person to Yvonne's deaf and deaf-blind friends. A few nights before her death, Marguerite Pitrois named several persons to whom she wanted to say her last farewells, and she asked Yvonne to tell the little deaf girls that she loved them very much.

Pitrois had feared the moment of her mother's death for a long time. When it finally arrived, she realized that she would have to live with the pain of no longer having her mother. She then turned this pain into an understanding of all who suffer. All that she did and wrote, from then on, would be in communion with her mother. She would seek to console all around her as her mother had done before her. It was a resolution that she would keep.

Pitrois outlined her plans for the future for her "little sisters." She would spend her winters with her sister, the director of a school in Chasseneuil, who had become a widow the previous year. They would sustain one another and her sister's son Jean through their mutual affection. In the summer she would go to a cottage near the sea in Brittany that she and her mother had owned. She planned to invite a number of her deaf "little sisters" to visit her seaside home. She hoped to bring them some happiness by providing them with a retreat that might help them to think and to find a new direction in life.

Even in her sorrow, Pitrois's commitment to her deaf and deaf-blind sisters remained strong, perhaps even stronger than before. Her mother was no longer there to second and support her writing. There was no question that Pitrois would continue writing and publishing *La Petite Silencieuse*. Thanking her subscribers for their numerous messages of sorrow upon her mother's death, she promised them a long issue within the next two months. It was a stunning triumph of courage and professionalism over personal pain.

Pitrois continued writing her journals and biographies, offering support to her deaf and deaf-blind friends and subscribers, and welcoming the most financially and psychologically needy among them into her home. Sadly, Pitrois was not blessed with a particularly long life. It was only a little more than a decade after the loss of her mother that she herself died, leaving behind many who mourned her.

Among these mourners was one of her reviewers and contemporaries, Harriet Montague, who recounted her sorrow at receiving notification of Pitrois's death in a letter edged with a black border. A leaflet was enclosed in the letter that said: "hélas, petites soeurs affligées, amies d'Yvonne Pitrois, *La Petite Silencieuse, Le Rayon de Soleil* ne vont plus paraître" ("alas, little afflicted sisters, friends of Yvonne Pitrois, *The Little Silent Girl, The Sunbeam* are no longer going to appear").[33] These unique periodicals had circulated largely through the generosity of Pitrois and her many friends and had brought peace and courage to hundreds, especially to the most neglected group, the deaf-blind community. But the periodicals would now be discontinued; they would not outlive their writer and editor. Her short biographical sketches in these periodicals, and her longer biographies reflecting the society within a society constituted by deaf and deaf-blind people, were her special province. No one else had the combination of knowledge and talent to duplicate her efforts.

Her understanding of what it meant to be deaf and blind had always motivated her writing. She wanted to help those with either or both of these disabilities, and, to that end, she created the equivalent of organizations for deaf and deaf-blind people in France, long before more prosperous and sophisticated organizations began. She preached internationalism and universal brotherhood to deaf people and spoke of the bonds of tenderness and empathy that united them everywhere, encouraging a spirit of mutual support and altruism. Her many challenges in life only served to strengthen her.

Supported by her mother, her faith, and her own creativity, and using her biographies as a way of coming to terms with her own deafness and with a temporary blindness that had, nonetheless left a permanent impression, Pitrois transcended her childhood trauma. She became a noteworthy force for good in her time, helping those most in need and developing into a writer and scholar who left, for future generations of deaf and hearing readers remarkable portraits of the deaf and deaf-blind communities of her age.

She was, all in all, an impressive individual. Yvonne Pitrois's biography of Abraham Lincoln was entitled *A Noble Life*. Montague wrote that this same title and characterization could be applied to the story of Pitrois's life—a life lived with dignity, charity, and a generous appreciation of the talented deaf contemporaries of her age.[34]

5 Corinne Rocheleau

Rescripting Life as a Deaf Woman

CORINNE ROCHELEAU (1881–1963), an accomplished Franco-American deaf feminist, essayist, and biographer, challenged the norms of early-twentieth-century society by the way in which she lived her life and by her adept chronicling of her own experience of marginality and that of others. Her biographies reflect her efforts to negotiate and expand the boundaries of her life and to reconnect in a creative way with the society at large.

Corinne Rocheleau wrote with an intuitive understanding of the principles that govern good biographical writing. She believed that biography should "reveal the individual within history and society."[1] Her portraits of early French female settlers of the New World (*Françaises d'Amérique*, 1915) carefully document the political and religious events that impacted the lives of the women. Similarly, in *Out of Her Prison* (1927), Rocheleau describes the situation of poor farmers in rural Canada and the limited opportunities for the education of deaf-blind people at the end of the nineteenth century to provide background and justification for the neglect experienced by her subject, Ludivine Lachance. Rocheleau pondered carefully the question of how biographers choose their subjects. Numerous times in the course of her career, she wrote that her own disability sensitized her to the suffering and challenges of others like herself, and this sensitivity led her to chronicle their experiences. Like biographers who followed her, particularly Edel and Maurois, the portrayal of this condition or characteristic led to a catharsis or transformation in her own life.[2] But as a deaf biographer, writing about deaf subjects and deafness, Rocheleau faced an additional challenge. She was doubly marginalized as both a woman and a deaf person. She used her writing to give voice to the "voiceless" subjects of her autobiographical essays and biographical studies. Whether dealing with the early Franco-American women settlers whose lives had been ignored by historians (*Françaises d'Amérique*) or writing of the retrieval, against all odds, of the deaf-blind Ludivine Lachance (*Hors de sa prison*), Rocheleau pursued her agenda of speaking for those who lacked power or were forgotten by society-at-large.

Rocheleau was born hearing, in 1881, in Rochester, Massachusetts, to a privileged Roman Catholic family. She was born on a Sunday, and her parents, who were extremely devout, wanted her christened at once. Her father wrapped her up, climbed into a streetcar, and headed to the parish church. Rocheleau, predictably, began to cry on this first, rather premature, journey. Hearing the timbre of the cry, the woman sitting near Mr. Rocheleau said, "This child seems to be a very young one, sir!" "Absolutely, madam," he answered; "she will be one day old tomorrow!"[3]

Rocheleau's French ancestors had immigrated to the New World centuries before and had been pioneers, either in Canada or in New England. Her parents were intellectuals, with artistic talents, and their home was filled with books, music, and paintings. The family got along harmoniously, as well. Until the age of nine, Rocheleau lived happily in her large family circle of parents and six brothers and sisters. Rocheleau described her father as "a real Lincoln!"[4] She worshipped him, and she admired her mother's charm and dedication to the family, although her relationship with her mother was more strained.

In her ninth year, she contracted mumps and the grippe, and as a result, she became deaf. In spite of good medical care, this progressive deafness could not be arrested by the best specialists in Boston and Worcester. Her deafness shattered her comfortable world of family stories shared as part of a large and loving household. In an autobiographical essay "My Education in a Convent School for the Deaf," she describes the trauma she underwent: "Along about my tenth year, then, my whole world would become out of joint and I had to adjust myself to the abnormal life of the deaf."[5]

Rocheleau tried unsuccessfully to keep up with the other children in the classroom and on the playground. She was then sent to a boarding school but felt isolated there, as well. Since she couldn't understand the speech of teachers and friends, she was given special lessons through writing. Because she was unhappy at school, her father would come and fetch her and bring her home. But then the parents, realizing that this was not a good situation for her, would send her back to school again. "So I began tacking back and forth like a buffeted sailboat in rough waters."[6]

Isolated at school, she was equally so at home. Rocheleau's family was musical, and she had had some piano lessons when she was very young. She now felt deprived of the music and the fellowship of the family gathered around the piano or organ while her mother played. She tried, at first, to keep up, but soon the effort to do so became futile: "as my hearing diminished, the hurt inside me grew, and I soon kept away from the musical groups and sat quietly on the arm of my father's chair, comforted by his deep, competent kindness, too proud to show my own hurt, and too conscious of my father's answering hurt to add to it in any way."[7]

In spite of the strong love of her father, Rocheleau's life became increasingly difficult. She realized that her voice and speech were disappearing. Her father and mother could no longer understand her and asked her to repeat things over and over again. She found herself needing to communicate with family and friends with paper, slate, and pencil. She began to avoid strangers and former playmates. Often she would escape to the home of an aunt or uncle across the lawn so that she wouldn't have to speak to visitors. Her father, alone, would seek her out and cajole her into joining the family circle and leaving her isolation.

The situation was hard for the parents, too, Rocheleau realized. The parents who had taken her to be christened on the first day of her life were both somewhat sustained by their religious faith. However, her mother believed that she should resign herself to her daughter's deafness, that it was her duty to do so. Conversely, her father's faith led him to find the best possible education for his daughter and to continue efforts to draw her out of her isolation and into the warmth of the family circle. He treated her like the other children and would not allow her to be pitied or spoiled. He disciplined her once in a while and encouraged her to go everywhere and to meet everyone. He tried, above all, to bolster her confidence and to cheer his sad daughter. Despite their different attitudes, neither parent abandoned the notion that Rocheleau's deafness could be cured. Twice weekly, her father took her to Boston for medical treatments, until it became evident that her hearing was not improving.

Unable to learn much at school or at home, one strong positive force in her life, in addition to the dedication of her father, was her omnivorous reading. She had learned to read while very young, and there were many books in the home. While other girls took their dolls with them everywhere, her own dolls were left neglected. But she would bring books to the table or to bed with her. To escape from her frustration and pain, she read prodigiously and broadly for a young teenaged girl. She read Shakespeare's plays, and the poems of Lamartine, Victor Hugo, Longfellow, and Byron. She read Racine's plays, Alcott's *Little Women*, and Dickens's *Oliver Twist*. She took in what she could of her reading, and much that she didn't yet understand would become clear later on. The reading had a healing effect on her, attenuating the shock of her deafness: "An abiding taste for good books was implanted in me, my active brain was fed, my imagination occupied, thereby helping me to retain perfect poise and sanity."[8]

But Rocheleau's parents needed to find more formal education for her, and, reluctantly abandoning their hope for a cure for their daughter, they sought a school for deaf children in which she could continue her studies. They wanted their daughter to be brought up in the Roman Catholic faith, and they wanted her to learn French and English, the two languages spoken fluently at home. Her father had already traveled to many state institutions and boarding schools for the deaf. The era was the 1890s, before the advent of day schools and public school classes for deaf children. What he had seen had not encouraged him. Eager for his daughter to regain her normal speech and her clear speaking voice, he noted that sign language was used as much as lipreading and speech training. It was not the path that he wanted for Corinne.

Finally, a relative spoke to her father of a priest, Canon Trépanier, who was head of the Montreal Institution for Deaf Girls in Montreal, Canada, a convent school run by the Sisters of Providence.* Rocheleau seemed instinctively to know, even at this first meeting, that she would be helped at this school. The canon, a tall, white-haired man with a kind face, rose to greet young Corinne and asked if she would like to attend a large school in Montreal where girls who were deaf, like herself, learned many things, including how to understand others and speak well. Corinne said immediately that she would like to go and that she wanted to leave at once, although she knew that Montreal was far away. She explains in her autobiographical essay "My Education in a Convent School for the Deaf" that she was moved by the "wise, understanding eyes" of Canon Trépanier and eager to accept his offer.[9]

The responses of her two parents to her choice were characteristically different from one another. Her father was pleased and surprised by her immediate acceptance, and he explained to her that she would have to wait a few months, until September, before classes began. Her mother, however, was upset that her daughter was entering a school for the deaf and decided to take matters into her own hands. The doctors had been puzzled and pessimistic. She could no longer turn to them for support. She turned, instead, to religion and prayer, particularly to Saint Anne. In a rare mischievous, almost impious remark, Rocheleau, a practicing Roman Catholic herself, observed that no amount of pilgrimages to Saint Anne altered the situation, "the good Saint Anne apparently being as deaf as the little girl she was implored for."[10]

Rocheleau felt that her mother had pity for her and saw her as a "case," which hurt Rocheleau's pride. Rocheleau believed that her burden was not one to be eliminated but to be borne. Everyone seemed to

---

* It is my understanding that Trépanier was in Massachusetts at the father's invitation, although that is not specifically stated. Her father had been seeking a school for Corrine, and she believed that there had been an exchange of letters between her father and the canon that soon led to the canon's arrival at the Rocheleau family's home.

have some burden, Rocheleau thought, and her deafness was not the worst possible one.

She left for the school at thirteen. At that point she felt like an overgrown little girl who was very sensitive to her own limitations. She was too proud to show how unhappy she was. Her father, alone, guessed it. She believed that his suffering for her was greater than her own for herself. The convent school would bring hope and possibility to them both. Rocheleau long remembered the first time she walked into this school. It looked to her like "a maze of halls and rooms."[11] It was an apt comparison, for Rocheleau needed to work her way through the maze of buildings in order to negotiate her deafness and reestablish connections between herself and her hearing family.

Several hundred people lived in the convent, lay people as well as clergy. The youngest students were about eight years old. There were also gray-haired longtime inhabitants for whom the convent had become a home. All took part in the varied activities of the convent, along with the sisters. Some of the students signed, while others spoke with great effort. All had very intense gazes as they tried to understand what was being communicated to them in sign or in spoken language. After four years at the convent school, Rocheleau attended a prep school with hearing students, took a course at a commercial school, studied at an art school, and took a year to travel and do research abroad in Europe. But the Montreal school had the most profound effect on her life.

Corinne Rocheleau developed quickly and well at the deaf school. After only one year, her teachers were elated at her progress, and her father was moved to tears. She could speak intelligibly and could understand him much more readily. She also had begun to learn to master the tinnitus, or head-noises, that had troubled her since the onset of her deafness. She learned to overcome this additional disability by the strength of her will.

During her first summer at home, she rejoined the society of the children and young people around her. "I was reinstated in the happy world of childhood from which I had been exiled during four or five miserable years."[12] She accepted this with joy for it enabled her to develop some necessary social skills. She still longed for her solitude and books occasionally, but she accepted all invitations to participate in the activities of family and friends. She understood, from her own experience, the need of the disabled to get beyond introspection and moodiness and to seek healthy diversions, and she also knew that her father found great happiness in seeing her play with girls of her age. Her efforts must have succeeded, for many years later an interviewer commented on her poise and charming manner.[13]

Rocheleau made excellent progress at the school. Her intelligence was quickly recognized by the nuns, who gave her a private tutor, but her skills were uneven. She could write letters both in French and English that amazed her teachers, but she had no knowledge of the rules of grammar or arithmetic. She studied very hard for three years. She spent one hour every day on English with Sister Ignatius Loyola, who worked with her on both spoken English and English grammar. The rest of her school day was devoted to various subjects taught her in French by Sister Ernestine.

Sister Ernestine taught her to reason out all her academic difficulties and motivated her so well that Rocheleau caught up quickly, making her way on her own through numerous textbooks. Rocheleau was still a child in many ways, however, and experienced some frustrations. She particularly hated arithmetic. One day, totally overwhelmed by cube roots, she sent her arithmetic book flying through an open window of the classroom! The firm Sister Ernestine told her to go out and pick it up again. She was then ordered to do two hours of cube roots instead of one hour. Although she didn't get the better of Sister Ernestine, Rocheleau later said that she got her vengeance on the field of mathematics by forgetting all that she had learned as soon as she left school.[14] But she valued Sister Ernestine's lessons in character development, all the same, as the sister tried to correct Rocheleau's dreaminess and independence, urging her to see that no person can stand alone and that thought should precede action.

The flexibility of the intellectual and moral training, tailored to each child, was not reflected in the convent's position on the oralism-manualism controversy. The most rigid rule of the institution was the line drawn between those using the oral method and those using the manual method. Speaking students couldn't use signs or mix with those who signed. Each group had assigned classrooms, dormitories, and recreation halls. Penalties were imposed upon those who disobeyed this rule. Rocheleau says that she soon saw the wisdom of the rule, because sign came more easily to the deaf students than spoken conversation. Even so, Rocheleau considered speech a superior mode of communication.

Although she admitted that sign offered far-reaching and swift communication, she still saw sign language as limited and even rudimentary. She was dedicated to the oral method that she had been taught. She saw sign as a system to be used only when the oral method failed with a student. Rocheleau wrote often and with pleasure of the fact that she had been praised for her voice and had been told that it was both normal and pleasant. She was told this not only in daily conversations but after numerous public lectures that she delivered. How did she manage to achieve such skill? Each year, Rocheleau would spend her vacations at the convent school, where, with the assistance of the nuns, she worked to perfect her speech and her voice. In midlife, she spoke of continuing to receive coaching once in a while. Such continued study, she felt, was necessary in order for a deaf person to maintain clear speech and a natural voice, both of which she saw as the only path by which a deaf person could have a "normal life."

Her dedication to oralism continued throughout her life. She most fully developed her thinking on this issue in an article she wrote in March of 1952 entitled "Mrs. Spencer Tracy Is Right: A Plea for Normal Education for the Deaf." The visits in February 1952 of Mrs. Tracy to Montreal and Toronto to discuss the work of her clinic, which supported oralism, led to much discussion and debate in French and English newspapers in these cities, inviting comments from notables like Dr. Leonard Elstad, then president of Gallaudet College, who wrote of the need for signs, based on the imprecision of lipreading.

Of particular interest in this article was Rocheleau's response to writ-

Corinne Rocheleau. Courtesy of the Sisters of Providence of the Deaf Institute in Montreal.

ten comments by a young deaf man of twenty-eight, named Donald Kidd, who had earned a Ph.D. from the University of Toronto. Kidd felt that only the combined system of signs, spelling, and some oral speech and lipreading could help a deaf child acquire language. Rocheleau, while admiring the accomplishments of Kidd, challenged this belief, asserting that her long experience had taught her that oral training enabled children to learn to write with more clarity and better grammar. She admitted to some exceptions but still felt, like Mrs. Tracy, that the oral method was best for the majority of deaf students. Sign, she asserted, should be used only by those unable to learn oral speech and lipreading after a trial period of reasonable duration.

Her objections were as much social as linguistic. She wanted for every deaf person a well-rounded life in society, and she felt that this could happen only if deaf people put themselves on an equal plane with hearing members of society. She did not see the need to adopt, unless completely necessary, a complex group of signals that might vary from country to country and be understood only by relatively few people. She felt that deaf people could make their mark only if they could understand others through lipreading and make themselves understood through oral speech. Rocheleau's major fear was that signs would segregate deaf people.

Perhaps remembering the pain of her own separation from family and friends after the onset of her deafness, Rocheleau wanted, above all, for deaf children to be able to connect with their parents and others close to them. She believed that signs set up a wall between the deaf people who used them and the public at large. But she was writing at a time when the issues of deaf people were not well understood and the idea of deaf people as a cultural minority had not yet developed. A half-century later, deaf activists are challenging the construct that deafness is a pathology or a deficit that must be overcome. They see it, instead, as a cultural phenomenon, based on linguistic differences.[15]

If she rejects signing, she does not reject the notion of living in a community in the service of deaf people. When she was a student at the Montreal school, a lesson from Sister Ernestine helped to instill in her lifelong principles of generosity and service. Once, in discussion with Sister Ernestine, Rocheleau was asked about heavenly blessings, or gifts from God. She thought first of small children, for whom she had a special fondness. But Sister Ernestine said that talents were also gifts from God and from parents, "and we must pass them on, if not directly, then through service and loving-kindness to those less fortunate than ourselves. It is another way to pass along the torch of life."[16]

This observation had a profound effect on her life, particularly since she saw it exemplified by the staff and teachers at the school. She deeply admired Canon Trépanier, who had devoted his life to the welfare of deaf people, as well as all of her teachers and all of the novices preparing for a similar vocation. The convent became a second home to her, as cherished as her New England home; the teachers and staff became a second family.

She felt both love and pity for her classmates, and she recognized her privileged position. Although many might have had more wealth, she believed that none had a father as wise as hers, nor as understanding a family. Other students lacked her motivation and pleasure in learning. Some, in fact, were truly unfortunate. Rocheleau tells the story of a girl named Alice, who was not very strong intellectually, but who had a kind heart. She grew very attached to Rocheleau and followed her around the convent with total devotion. Rocheleau, pitying Alice's lack of family and admiring her gentleness, gave her time and attention in turn. When Alice died, according to the nuns in the infirmary, she had Rocheleau's last letter under her pillow. In *Hors de sa prison*, Rocheleau tells an even more heartrending tale of a deaf-blind classmate.

Her other classmates were as wonderful as Alice in their steadfast friendship. She tried to offer them a taste of the world outside and showed them, in turn, how much she appreciated their contributions within the convent walls. Many of her classmates became nuns. Others were unmarried and lived, sometimes by choice, sometimes by necessity, in the convent. Still others had been cast off by their families: the lame, the unattractive, the dozen or so who were blind as well as deaf. Rocheleau revered her teachers, who created a home in the convent for all of them.

Rocheleau loved all of the activities in the house, including the household tasks. She would be absorbed over the drawing board, trying to make buttonholes in the sewing room or taking cooking lessons among the huge pans in the kitchen. This sharing of responsibilities among teachers and students led to a profound sense of community. Kept busy both inside and outside the classroom, the four years of her stay at the Montreal convent sped by very quickly. She was always eager to go home for vacations and eager to come back to school throughout that period.

The Montreal school, with its intellectual and moral training, gave Rocheleau the skills to function on a broader stage than that of private domestic life. Her recounting of this training and its impact on her life in "My Education in a Convent School for the Deaf," an essay that might be called a memoir today, reveals a woman ahead of her time. According to Heilbrun, it is not until the 1990s that women write of their spiritual and intellectual development, of a desire to find a place to function in the world in which one can develop and use one's skills and talents.[17] The convent school had gone beyond helping her deal with her deafness. It gave her the confidence and skills to begin to define a larger place for herself in society.

In the first seven years after her return home, however, she had reason to be grateful for the domestic training that had been part of the curriculum. Her mother had died while she was still in Montreal, and at the age of nineteen, she lost her beloved father. Rocheleau devoted herself to caring for her two younger sisters, trying to be both mother and father to them as they pursued their studies. She stayed with her sisters until they became independent and had homes of their own. It was only after this that she pursued her own career path. She was ready to strike out on her own, but she also needed to find a way to support herself, as the income left by Rocheleau's father had dwindled. Some members of the family criticized this bold move, while others were more understanding. Ignoring all commentary, Rocheleau took the Civil Service examination and passed it brilliantly, earning an appointment as a clerk in the Research Division of the United States Census Bureau in Washington, D.C. She lived there alone for two years, occupied by her job responsibilities. Throughout this stay, Rocheleau haunted the libraries, driven by her passion for learning. She liked the work and the city but her health, always frail, worsened in Washington, which was too hot for a person who had been a northerner. She was forced to rethink her options.

With some hesitation, she accepted her brother's offer to come back to Worcester and become his associate in the family business. He was the owner of a chain of stores across all of New England, and her job was to assist him in the management of a clothing warehouse. She had complete responsibility for the office, including correspondence, calculation, money matters, and bookkeeping. In her brother's absence, she also managed the employees. She made a good living from this job and acquired a great deal of experience. The tasks were difficult for her only because her heart was elsewhere. She confessed in an interview with Yvonne Pitrois that "frankly, this life of a business woman is the last one that I would have chosen."[18] Nonetheless, she succeeded in this enterprise as well as in all others that she undertook.

She further challenged what was considered acceptable behavior for women, particularly for deaf women, by traveling to Europe in 1921, accompanied by a friend. She did an eight-month tour of France, Italy, Belgium, Switzerland, Spain, and England. She had intended to visit many schools for the deaf in Europe, but a broken ankle kept her in Venice for two months. Always brave and determined, she finished her trip, leaning on a cane, and still managed to see four deaf schools: two in Switzerland, the National Institute in Paris, and the school for deaf and blind girls in Larnay, near Poitiers, France.

The trip inspired her to write, as the visits to the deaf schools would later inspire her thoughtful work in the area of curriculum development for deaf students. From Europe, she sent articles to the *Revue Canadienne*, under the title "Letters from Corinne." Once back in America, she gave two lectures in Montreal of a literary and religious nature, entitled "Rome" and "Lourdes." According to Pitrois, on page 7 of her interview entitled "Corinne Rocheleau," she delivered these lectures personally in a highly successful manner.

Even during these busy years, Rocheleau managed to find moments of peace in her life and joy in the society of others. She continued to use reading as a path to self-knowledge and knowledge of the world. She was a member of the Alliance Française, a group still in existence today, that promotes Franco-American activities and friendship. She was the founding member of the "Cercle Jeanne Mance" (the Jeanne Mance Circle) of which she had also been the secretary and vice president. The Circle was a Franco-American literary and social society. She was a member of the Business and Professional Women's Guild and of Saint Agnes' Guild, which supported a home for young Catholic girls. During this time, her life was pleasant and interesting. For seventeen years she balanced her career as a reluctant businesswoman with reading, cultural activities, and her own writing. In 1929, however, the firm closed its doors, after a half century of existence, and Rocheleau found that she could devote herself more completely to her writing.

Rocheleau's life took another unexpected turn a year later. In Washington, D.C., she had met Wilfrid Rouleau, a scholar and linguist. As they got to know one another better, a deep affection and friendship developed between them, and they made plans to marry in August of 1930. They married in the private chapel of the cathedral of Montreal in the course of a religious ceremony over which Monsignor Alphonse Deschamps presided. He was the auxiliary bishop of Montreal and the former chaplain of the deaf school, and Rocheleau had deeply admired him when she was a student there.

Then the couple returned to Washington for a few years. There she kept house, enjoyed the capital's libraries and museums, and served as chair of a committee at the Volta Bureau. Above all, she continued to write, encouraged by her husband. In doing this, she challenged the accepted view that women could either have public lives and not marry or have private lives as married women and not be professionals. Rocheleau often spoke of the happiness of her years of marriage. This happiness is discussed by Corrine Rocheleau in the interview that she has with Dion-Lévesque and also in many other sources. She enjoyed having her own home and garden in the city of Washington, and the life she and Wilfrid created there. She had all the friends and books she desired. Sadly, the marriage lasted only a decade. Wilfrid Rouleau became ill and died in 1940. Again, Rocheleau had to rethink her options. She and her husband had taken up residence temporarily at the Montreal Institution for Deaf Girls so that she could conduct research and write. The directors of the school had asked her to develop a lecture series for teachers of the deaf focusing on the history of deaf education across the globe. After a trip to settle some business matters, she decided to take up permanent residence in the lay quarters of the school. She continued to do research and writing in support of deaf education and, in her later years, was particularly active in the Social Services Division of the institution.

Corinne Rocheleau took pride in her achievements, although she modestly tended to attribute them to her training and perseverance. She possessed a flexibility that enabled her to move beyond trauma to ever new areas of life. Her work as a biographer best reflects her dual interests in women's issues and deaf issues and her efforts to respond to the challenges that both groups had in living their lives as respected members of society.

ROCHELEAU'S FRANCO-AMERICAN heritage and her commitment to chronicling women's history is clearly revealed in *Françaises d'Amérique* (*Heroic French Women of Canada*, 1915). This collection of the lives and deeds of heroic women settlers of Canada surprises by its form, as well as by its content. Each chapter portrays the life of one or two individual women, although the lives of the women throughout the book are often interconnected, and the chapters double as short, dramatic scenes. This biography was, in fact, performed as a play under the auspices of the Jeanne Mance Circle, the Franco-American cultural group that Rocheleau had helped to found. Its first production was on February 10, 1915.

Françaises d'Amerique illustrates Maurois's belief that the life of the writer and that of her heroes or subjects often coincide, at least to some extent. In these moments, what we have is "autobiography disguised as biography."[19] Rocheleau is, of course, exploring her own past in this work. She dedicated the book to all Franco-American women, with whom she felt a particular bond. In her preface she explains that male French colonists were much written about, but their female counterparts were ignored. Rocheleau hoped to bring them out of the realm of the forgotten. This was not an easy task, for the centuries had almost erased these women's footsteps from American soil.

Proving herself a dedicated historian, she sought out old registries in Quebec, Montreal, Detroit, and New Orleans to find the names of these heroines and to learn their destinies. The more she read, the more she became committed to portraying their charm, Gallic boldness, and spirit. Her sister, Albani Rocheleau-Brodeur, provided beautiful sketches for the text that helped to highlight the individual personalities and paths chosen by the women. In this retelling of individual destinies, Rocheleau goes beyond exploring the past to envisioning the future for herself and for other women of her era. She records and analyzes the unusual options chosen by women arriving in the New World who often were called upon to perform tasks and roles generally reserved for men in their country of origin.

Among the rich stories in the collection is the sketch of "Madame Hébert and Her Daughter, Guillemette." At first glance it seems to be a fairly conventional portrait of a mother devoted to her family and her faith. But by using the device of a conversation between the mother and daughter to tell the story of this first colonial family to arrive in Canada, Rocheleau traces for us the courage and initiative of a woman who chose to accompany her husband to the New World, rather than to wait for him in France. Hébert braved a winter crossing that took three months. When the family arrived in Quebec, they found primitive conditions and endured attacks by the English that deprived them of their autonomy and their Catholic faith. Under these difficult circumstances, Madame Hébert sustained not only her own family but the other settlers. When others in the colony did not have enough food, she shared her own food with them. Three years later, Canada became French again, and Hébert offered her home for the celebration of the first Mass since the English occupation.

Although Madame Hébert appears to be a conventional woman in her roles as wife and mother, she extended the traditional maternal role to serve as mother to the entire colony. She offered food and hospitality to all who needed it. As the sketch concludes, Hébert's daughter Guillemette underlines this point. Although things are more peaceful now politically, Guillemette says, her mother still works very hard taking care of all the abandoned Indian children. She is known as the godmother of all of Quebec. Hébert responds to the teasing by saying, "Ma fille, c'est une belle mission, va, que de servir de mère à toute une colonie!"("My daughter, it's a fine mission, come along now, to serve as mother to a whole colony!")[20]

Rocheleau's chapter on Madame de La Tour relates the life and death of Marie Jacquelin, the wife of Charles de La Tour, commander of Fort La Tour in Acadia. The de La Tours were Huguenots and, as such, were trusted neither by the French Catholics nor by the English, who saw them as French subjects. Their major enemy, however, was their neighbor de Charnisay. The cowardly de Charnisay attacked during the absence of Charles de La Tour but met fierce resistance from Madame de La Tour, who led her husband's troops. Only the betrayal of one of her men led to her defeat during de Charnisay's third attack, in 1647.

In the imagined dialogue Madame de La Tour has with a lady companion after the battle, she expresses her sense of shame. Although she had fought nobly and only lost through betrayal and ruse, she still feels disgraced by the loss and doesn't want her husband to see her in defeat. She died of sadness and chagrin ten days after the seizing of the fort's tower. We see here a woman assuming the role of warrior and, along with it, the heroic sense of honor and duty that a man of the period might have shown.

Another of the portraits differs dramatically from these first two. It is the biographical study of Jeanne le Ber, who was known as the "saintly recluse." Le Ber was born in Montreal of parents who had come from Normandy, and she was the goddaughter of Jeanne Mance, who played an important part in the establishment of Montreal. In Rocheleau's sketch, Jeanne le Ber is with her cousin. Throughout the scene, Jeanne doesn't speak, rather her cousin tells her story. The cousin recounts that from an early age, Le Ber had an inclination toward solitude and silence, although she was gracious and capable of talking with charm and facility. She disdained rich food and clothing, though these were easily provided by her wealthy merchant father.

Le Ber's parents were eager to see their daughter well established in the country, so her father chose a husband for her when she left the convent school. She refused, however, to receive this man and expressed her desire to live in a state of retreat. Her parents accepted, hoping this would be a temporary choice, but that was not the case. Le Ber locked herself in her room in her parents' house for fifteen years, leaving only to attend Mass at 5:00 A.M., accompanied by her cousin. She communicated with her family through her cousin. Neither her mother's last malady and death nor her brother's death in combat against the English could persuade her to abandon her solitude.

Le Ber wanted still more isolation. In order not to have to leave her home for Mass, she offered money to the Sisters of the Congregation of Notre Dame for the building of a chapel, provided that it contain an apartment in which she could live. The sisters accepted her offer. Le Ber's apartment had three austere living spaces. In the first, she embroidered many objects for the altar. She was gifted in this art. In the second cell she kept her straw bed. In the third cell, which was separated from the chapel by a grill, she attended Mass without leaving her quarters or being seen.

Jeanne divided her day between work, meditation, and prayer. At midnight, she would enter the empty chapel and pray before the altar. Although she never became a nun, she took a vow of perpetual life in a convent, a decision that was very difficult for her father, who was permitted to see her only twice a year. She was not at her father's deathbed but she watched his funeral service from her cell.

Le Ber's example was felt from afar, although she lived withdrawn from the world. Two Protestant ministers, having heard her story from the bishop while passing through Montreal, were deeply affected by it. One even converted to Catholicism, moved to embrace a religion that could inspire such a life of sacrifice. Jeanne le Ber had renounced everything that women of her age sought—home, family, friendships, a life of comfort, and even "the voice" that women were learning to use to determine their own lives. But here it could be argued that Le Ber's was an eloquent silence that underscored her extreme devotion to her faith.

THESE FASCINATING, disparate, portraits are not only depictions of historical figures but symbolic representations of aspects of Rocheleau's personality that she exhibited during the course of her life. The maternal principle, illustrated by Madame Hébert, would be revealed in her relationships with her nieces and nephews and the children in the convent school for the deaf. The strength of the warrior, illustrated by Madame de La Tour, would be reflected in Rocheleau's courage in fighting for a larger place for women in society and for the rights of deaf children to a better education. Rocheleau's contemplative side, reflected in the story of Jeanne le Ber, would be seen in Rocheleau's desire to finish her days in quarters in the convent.

In writing *Françaises d'Amérique*, Rocheleau began to define the qualities that she valued and that had the potentiality to expand the parameters of her life. She linked this personal quest to her desire to record Franco-American history. She was seen as an ambassador of Franco-American culture in North America and abroad, where her writing and work as an educator were deeply admired. The Franco-Americans recognized and honored Rocheleau's talent. She received the much coveted Medal of Honor from the Franco-American Historical Society of Boston. Throughout her adult life she remained concerned about the survival of this subculture, which she wanted to keep separate and intact. She believed the culture would survive, as long as parishes, schools, and French language societies endured. She was against the notion of a "melting pot" that would inevitably lead to the loss of the French language and the French character of the community. This concern differs very radically from her view of deaf people and deafness, for she believed that deaf people should be integrated into the society at large whenever possible.

Rocheleau maintained her insistence on integration for deaf people even in her discussion of the severely disabled Ludivine Lachance in *Hors de sa prison*. What impelled Rocheleau to write a biography of the deaf-blind Lachance? In part, Rocheleau reflected Edel's view that the biographer's inner life and desires will lead him or her to choose a particular subject. Although her own disability was deafness alone, Rocheleau stated in "My Education in a Convent School for the Deaf" that it gave her empathy for all those who had physical limitations of any kind, particularly children, whom she saw as the most vulnerable. She developed a specialty in the field of the deaf-blind, believing that this field, at that time referred to as the "Helen Keller cases," was too little understood. She researched this population extensively both in Europe and in America and published not only *Hors de sa Prison* (1927) but also *Those in the Dark Silence* (with Rebecca Mack) in 1930.

Hors de sa prison was the most widely praised of Rocheleau's works. It was one of the most highly regarded works of its day on the education of deaf-blind people, and its first edition sold out.

THE NAME of the deaf-blind Canadian girl, Ludivine Lachance, is certainly an ironic one. "La chance" in French means "luck," but Ludivine's life was short and sad. She was born in 1895 to poor farming people who lived at a forest's edge in a Canadian district with nearly impassable roads and sparsely placed houses. She was born with all of her senses and had begun to talk, when, between the ages of two and three, she contracted meningitis. She recovered from the illness, but the high fever caused her to become both deaf and blind. Within a few weeks, she had also forgotten how to speak.

Her parents loved her, but they were sadly ignorant and perplexed as to how to care for her. They worked outdoors all day long, so to help their daughter avoid accidents, they shut her in a narrow room, a virtual closet with no window. The only opening was a door that was always kept locked. As there was little air in the room, she put her mouth to the cracks between the boards and breathed in the wind. Her sole occupation was to walk forward and back for hours in her "cell," making animal-like noises. Finally, she would be exhausted and go to her bed, falling on it into a heavy sleep. The bed was the single piece of furniture in the room that she did not break in a fit of anger. She wore no shoes, and her only clothing was a shapeless bag that she refused to change.

Lachance's contact with her parents was woefully limited. When they returned from farming, they would give her food. She would grab it from their hands and devour it like an animal. They would caress her for a while and then, used to this strange life, she would return to her cell. Lachance spent thirteen years in this closet, leaving it, finally, when she was sixteen.

The neighbors pitied the Lachance's bad luck in having this monster of a child, but they could offer little advice or help. Only the vicar of the parish knew there was a better way to deal with this child. He was aware of the Montreal Institution for Deaf Girls, run by the Sisters of Providence, and he was certain that, out of faith and mercy, they would receive Ludivine. For many years, the parents refused to be separated from their child. They did not trust convents and feared that the nuns might harm their child. In reality, when the Sisters of Providence heard of the unfortunate Ludivine from the priest, they sent two of the sisters to France to learn how to teach Ludivine, just in case her parents released her to their care. The two nuns went to Notre Dame de Larnay, the school for deaf girls near Poitiers, and they stayed for a year, learning methods of teaching deaf-blind children.

The chaplain of the Montreal school went twice to the Lachances to try to overcome their opposition to Ludivine's attending the convent school. After the second visit, in June of 1911, he finally succeeded and was able to tell the nuns to come for their student. The sisters were shocked by Ludivine's appearance; she barely seemed human. They used caresses, fruits, and sweets to try to tame her. She touched the nuns' faces and felt in their pockets for sweets, but when they tried to dress her in preparation for the trip to Montreal, she began to scratch them and howl. In fact, it took them a week to get Ludivine on the train to Montreal, and the trip was harrowing, with much screaming on the part of Ludivine. With Ludivine finally out of her closet prison, the sisters wondered whether they would be able to bring her out of the prison of ignorance, solitude, and silence. Touch needed to be the main vehicle for instruction, but Ludivine was hampered in that manner, as well. She rarely used her hands; in fact, they were practically useless for that reason. She could pick things up only with her thumb and forefinger. The school physician was rather pessimistic and told the sisters that their task was hopeless.

But the sisters had a great interest in her and great patience with her. Sister Angélique was chosen to be her spiritual mother and teacher and completely dedicated herself to the task. Ludivine was led everywhere by her and others to feel her new surroundings—the people, the rooms, the furniture. It was an amazing change for her after her restricted life in the small closet. Her first lessons, slow in the learning, were of a physical nature, learning how to wash herself and how to eat decently. The next group of lessons focused on communication. The first expressed idea she was taught was how to learn to spell on her hand the letter "o," to ask for an egg ("oeuf" in French). It took Ludivine three days to understand the sign, to make it herself, and to receive the egg. After that one sign came many more. And once she could communicate, even in a rudimentary way, she was no longer hostile, and she eventually evolved into a gentle girl who used signs and read and wrote in Braille and raised letters.

Lachance became adept at making things with her hands. After her death, the school museum exhibited some 150 objects that she had made, including wicker and rush cane baskets, silk bookmarks, frames, and cushions. Most impressively, she was motivated to work on her own. Once her teacher left her for a few hours and gave her some cloth, thread, a needle, and scissors. Although the teacher had given Ludivine no instructions, when she returned she was amazed to see that Ludivine had made a dress for her doll, and one that reflected the latest fashion. Lachance's most impressive gains, however, came in her awareness of morality and religion. She had been an imprisoned soul for sixteen years, but after a short time in the convent she revealed great qualities of heart. She grew to love the sisters, particularly her two teachers, Sister Angélique-Marie and Sister Ildefonse, the deaf nun who acted as her underteacher and companion. She loved her parents who came to visit her every year and who were happy and moved to tears by the transformation in their daughter. She also developed a deep sense of spirituality and evidenced radiance when she prayed.

But the conditions in which she had lived led her to be tubercular. In spite of the good care she received from the sisters, her health declined, and she died in the spring of 1918, at the age of twenty-four. Although she had greatly feared death, which the sisters had explained to her during a visit to the churchyard, when her time came, she accepted death peacefully, thanking and embracing her teachers and kissing a cross. It was death that ultimately released her from the prison of her multiple disabilities and illnesses.

LUDIVINE LACHANCE and her spiritual regeneration against all odds are clearly the heart of Rocheleau's biography. However, Rocheleau sets Lachance's life within the context of the history of the education of the deaf and deaf-blind. She begins with Laura Bridgman, the first deaf-blind person to be educated in the United States. Bridgman was born in 1829 in New Hampshire, and she was discovered by Samuel Gridley Howe, director of the Perkins Institution for the Blind in Boston. Howe brought her to the school, and she remained there for the rest of her life. Rocheleau also writes about Helen Keller, whose education by Anne Sullivan was and is still the most impressive story of the education of a deaf-blind person. Rocheleau also recounts the work of the sisters of Larnay, who had educated numerous deaf-blind girls, including Marie Heurtin, a particularly gifted student. Sister Angélique-Marie read about all of these prior efforts before she attempted the education of Ludivine, who presented a more challenging situation because of her deprived childhood. Rocheleau praises the Sisters of Providence and the clergy of the convent for the strong sense of vocation and spirit of charity that moved all who lived and worked in the house.

At the end of *Hors de sa prison*, Rocheleau discusses teaching methodology, makes some suggestions for teachers of the deaf, and delivers a powerful plea for cooperation among institutions serving deaf and deaf-blind children. Always interested in new ways to instruct deaf children, Rocheleau concludes that the best method is always the one most suited to the individual student. For Ludivine Lachance, this meant learning a few signs and the manual alphabet, and this was enough to open her world. Strongly asserting that deaf and deaf-blind children have the same capabilities as other children, Rocheleau insists that their teachers be well trained. The teachers must inculcate in disabled children good judgment and character and self-confidence. They must focus on the strengths of their students, rather than on their weaknesses. In order to learn to do so, teachers of the disabled must read relevant literature, visit institutions in their own country and abroad, and attend conferences that keep them apprised of current systems and technologies.

Above all else, Rocheleau believes in the value of cooperation. Each institution has a special strength that could benefit the others, so cooperation could lead to further excellence, according to Rocheleau. The practical life lessons taught at Larnay, the modern intellectual education offered at Saint-Louis and Gallaudet College, and the family spirit and excellence in speech training offered at the Montreal Institution for Deaf Girls, if combined, would give the deaf student a complete education. She hopes for this as well as for the time when disabled people receive the consideration due them, no more nor less than this, as she puts it. At that time, she feels, an intelligent understanding will replace a facile pity that is both unnecessary and unhelpful. Then we will know, she believes, that the human race has taken a gigantic step forward.

Thus, Rocheleau's biography of Ludivine Lachance goes beyond the discussion of one person's life to a strikingly modern analysis of the issues and concerns in the education of the deaf and deaf-blind of Rocheleau's era, many of which we still struggle with today. If she did not have all the answers, she certainly courageously set forth the problems and hoped we would have a similar courage in responding to her challenges.

In contrast to Couser's claim that disability narratives are often not artful, Corinne Rocheleau, wrote biographies that are both artful and socially useful.[21] She was ahead of her time in reducing stigma and marginalization for deaf women. She finds meaning and healing in the telling of her tales. While some people fear that an illness or disability will render their lives meaningless, coherent narratives by and about disabled people can strengthen and add value to all lives.[22] A reader can learn empathy and courage from Rocheleau's characters, who are always noble, even when faced with difficult futures.

A unique feature of Rocheleau's work is her dual emphasis on the reclamation of women as subjects and her use of her writing to try to improve the conditions of deaf people and of women. Carolyn Heilbrun maintains that autobiographical writing offers women the greatest opportunity to write about being between worlds. It also allows women to discover and recreate themselves. Newer memoirs allow inclusion of a goal, ambitions, and the suffering women have experienced trying to make their way in society. These newer memoirs don't have the apologetic tone of earlier female autobiography.[23] One remarkable aspect of Rocheleau's contributions is that her work as a memoirist in "My Education in a Convent School for the Deaf" and as a biographer in *Françaises d'Amérique . . .* and *Hors de sa prison* is honest in its portrayal of suffering and obstacles, but it refuses to allow women to be victims. This is rare in such early work. For women, as for deaf people, Rocheleau believes that the key is to find a voice.

Rocheleau viewed her deafness as a personal condition, rather than a cultural one, but in her essay "My Education in a Convent School for the Deaf," she writes movingly of the impact of her deafness on her life. It is a disability for her, but one over which she triumphs through hard work, learning to lipread and relearning speech, and overcoming her bitterness with the aid of the nuns and through the medium of her writing. She exemplifies the oralist ideal of restoring the deaf to society, that is, the deaf person who has overcome a so-called handicap and is successfully integrated into the world of hearing people.[24]

Rocheleau saw herself as a person who overcame a major disability. Though her disability could not be cured, she was able to live a good life anyway. She believed that "a normal, fruitful, even happy life may result therefrom, through the right sort of training and guidance during childhood and adolescence."[25] She saw her writing as a way to serve. She let it be the instrument of her heart, and tried to better the lives of deaf and blind people by means of her craft.

She received an impressive number of awards for her writing. In 1928 the French Academy awarded her a gold medal for *Hors de sa prison*, and in 1929, Pope Pius XI, through his secretary, Cardinal Gaspari, sent a letter of congratulations for this same book. In 1947 the Franco-American Historical Society of Boston gave her its medal of honor. She was the only woman to receive it in the fifty years that the society had existed. In 1949 she was elected member for life in the Gallery of Living Catholic Authors.

Rocheleau was an exceptional deaf biographer and autobiographer. She remained cognizant of her standing as an early-twentieth-century woman and how that intersected with her deafness. Her dedication to the deaf and deaf-blind community was impressive. She wrote in support of broader opportunities for them to live their lives to the fullest. Her return to the convent to spend the last years of her life writing curricula for teachers of the deaf and her work in the Social Services Division of the convent reflected her deep desire to serve deaf people and to live in the deaf community of the convent school, which became her second home. Whether we accept or challenge her view of deafness as a disability, her dedication to her work in support of the deaf community and her writings chronicling and critiquing the marginality of women, of deaf people, and of deaf-blind people, commend her to our interest and study as we continue to reflect on many of the concerns she raised in her excellent biographical studies.

6 *Biography in Deaf Hands*

An Analysis

With the exception of Corinne Rocheleau, none of the writers discussed in this volume wrote autobiographical narratives. Certainly there was a lack of deaf autobiographical models in the nineteenth and early twentieth centuries. But does this alone explain why Jean-Ferdinand Berthier, Yvonne Pitrois, and Corinne Rocheleau did not write about their own lives?

Berthier indicated several times that he planned to write an autobiographical essay, but he never did so.* However, through the letters and the biographies he wrote, we get insight into his perception of his own life and times. His deep friendship for Bébian, his former teacher, expresses itself in his mournful commentary that Bébian died in sadness, far away from the deaf friends at the Paris institute who would have wanted to help and sustain him through these difficult hours.[1] Berthier's personal reverence for the Abbé de l'Épée is revealed throughout the text of his biography of the abbé (*L'Abbé de l'Épée, Sa Vie, Son Apostolat, Ses Travaux, Ses Luttes et Ses Succès . . .*), particularly in his citing of the abbé's understanding that deaf people, above all, needed to have their dignity respected.[2]

Yvonne Pitrois did not write any sort of autobiographical statement either. Perhaps her shyness, coupled with her deep religiosity as a

---

* On page 13 of volume 2 of *Aux Origines du movement sourd: Ferdinand Berthier (1803–1886)*, edited by Yves Delaporte, we are informed that in 1861, at the same time that Berthier was seeking a number of more elevated posts, including that of archivist, he was also actively planning to write an autobiography. The projected title was *Les Mémoires d'un sourd-muet*, but this work was never completed.

devout Protestant, made such an essay seem exhibitionistic or self-promoting to her. Indeed, in a 1928 essay about Pitrois's later years, Margaret Hance speculated that temperamental reluctance was to blame for the absence of a Pitrois autobiography.[3] Hance encouraged others to fill the void and write about this woman who never wrote about herself, but essays about Pitrois are all too rare, and much remains to be learned about this highly intelligent, gifted woman who devoted herself to her deaf and deaf-blind contemporaries.

We can piece together some of her views and aspects of her personality from her biographical studies and her personal commentary in *La Petite Silencieuse* (*The Little Silent Girl*). From Hance we learn the staggering information that Pitrois did not personally meet another deaf girl until she was seventeen, and only then did she fully understand that her difference was shared by many others in France and across the world.[4] Pitrois used her newsletter to offer succor and support to deaf women.[5] In writing essays and articles for the magazine, she lost the feeling of isolation that her disability had imposed upon her, and she became a dear friend to the deaf "little sisters" who read her magazine and corresponded with her. But, equally important, Pitrois revealed her personal life in the magazine and shared it with her readers. One of the most touching issues included an account of her grief at the death of her mother and her plans to live part of each year, henceforth, with her older sister and nephew.[6] It is a somewhat brief, truncated autobiographical narrative, but it is the only kind that Pitrois allowed herself.

Pitrois's biographies also include her personal views. In chapter 2 of her biography of Helen Keller, she expressed her belief that Keller's appearances on the vaudeville stage were demeaning to the image of a deaf-blind person. Pitrois recommended that Keller find a more dignified manner of presenting herself to the hearing world. Pitrois's austere religiosity was clearly revealed through this commentary, although she did not express her views in the first person.

Corinne Rocheleau produced a clear narrative of the onset of her deafness in "My Education in a Convent School for the Deaf." She wrote of the losses her deafness introduced into her life and her subsequent reclamation of much that she had lost—family, friends, and a joy in living. Her years at the deaf school in Montreal nurtured her love of art, letters, and scholarship and taught her to feel less bitter about her problems interacting with hearing society. As with Berthier and Pitrois, her biographies offer her personal perspectives, as well.

Rocheleau's boundless respect for the nuns who educated her was revealed in her narrative *Hors de sa prison* (*Out of Her Prison*), an account of the spiritual awakening of Ludivine Lachance, the deaf-blind girl who evolved from an animal-like creature to a gentle, sweet-tempered girl. The same nuns who educated Corinne Rocheleau educated Lachance, and Rocheleau recognized that Lachance learned to communicate because of the nuns' love, skill, and dedication.

Berthier, Pitrois, and Rocheleau used the genre of biography as a way of depicting the people and the world they inhabited, explaining not only for posterity but for themselves, what their life experience had been and what it meant. All three writers had been wounded by hearing society, whether intentionally or otherwise, and they were wise enough to know that they needed to find a place of comfort in both worlds. This theme of bridging the gap between the deaf and the hearing worlds is central to the work of these three deaf biographers and unique to them in the form it takes.

Berthier used his successive works on Bébian, the Abbé de l'Épée, and the Abbé Sicard to find a way out of the loss of his post and his dignity when the rotation system was imposed on deaf instructors at the Paris Institution for the Deaf. This strategy helped him to defuse his anger enough to become a brilliant teacher and a political force throughout his life.

Pitrois was able to free herself from the haunting memory of days in a dark room, fearing her sight would never return, by telling the stories of blind men and women who led productive lives. She created newsletters for deaf and blind people and, in the years following the death of her mother, welcomed into her home young deaf and deaf-blind women who sought direction in their lives.

Rocheleau came to terms with her life as a deaf person and as a woman by writing biographies. Her sketches of heroic women in *Françaises d'Amérique* (*Heroic French Women of Canada*) gave her models of courage that fortified her in her own life. The biography of Ludivine Lachance (*Hors de sa prison*) sends the profoundly hopeful message that love, devotion, and a measure of skill can unlock even the most uneducated, neglected mind.

Rocheleau, by her own admission, felt bitter at the loss of her hearing at the age of nine. She gradually developed a more optimistic view of society and a belief that she could have a more positive relationship to it. In later years, she had a full social life through her marriage to Wilfrid Rouleau, and she conducted research and wrote at the Montreal Institution for Deaf Girls where she, herself, had been educated. She found satisfaction in both her personal and professional lives.

These biographers, then, had a common need to address and to heal the traumas they had experienced. This need led them to perceive and then cross the divide between themselves and hearing society. Through the characters they portrayed in their biographies, they found a way to heal themselves and to build a bridge back to the society at large in order to find personal and professional fulfillment.

At the same time, they belonged to a community within a community and had to define their views of themselves as deaf individuals and their positions on the language that should be used by the deaf community. Berthier loved sign language, he believed it was the only way to teach deaf children, and he saw it as a powerful political and artistic language that bound the members of the deaf community. He revered Auguste Bébian, a hearing man who knew sign language as well as any deaf person, and the Abbé de l'Épée, who saw its potential as a way of educating deaf children. Berthier fought for the use of sign language at the Paris Institution for the Deaf throughout his life and considered every suppression of it as a tragedy. Pitrois, although somewhat acquainted with signs and fingerspelling, wrote in her article, "The National Institution for the Deaf in Paris," that the oral instruction then in use at the institution was one reason for the teaching success there.[7]

Rocheleau was far more militant in her support of oralism. She stated numerous times that sign was only for those who could not succeed with the oral method. She believed that oral training alone enabled deaf children to learn grammar and to learn to write with clarity. Her objections to sign were social as well as linguistic. She thought that signs would segregate deaf people from mainstream society, and she wanted every deaf person to experience a complete life in society.[**]

These different perspectives make sense to us when we realize that Berthier was educated and worked at a time when sign language was still prevalent in France. Pitrois and Rocheleau had little occasion to see signs or to compare its results with those of oralism. They were both educated after the participants of the Congress of Milan had banned sign language in schools for the deaf, and their opinions, of necessity, were influenced by this situation.

Despite their divergent views, all three biographers were dedicated to serving the deaf population. Crossing the divide did not mean ignoring their own affiliation with the deaf community. Berthier wanted to serve the twenty-two thousand French deaf people of his era by teaching them their rights and their cultural history. His biographies portray the lives of the French deaf intellectual elite at the National Institute for the Deaf. He traces their struggles, triumphs, and defeats and their interaction with hearing allies.

Pitrois, in her periodicals for the deaf and deaf-blind community, *La Petite Silencieuse* and *Le Rayon de Soleil*, respectively, and in her biographical studies, including those of Helen Keller, Louis Braille, Maurice de la Sizeranne, and the deaf-blind students at Larnay, recreates the society within a society that the deaf and deaf-blind community constituted and tries to tell her stories with a moral end in view. Each biographical portrait offers the reader a lesson in persistence, courage, and

---

[**] Rocheleau's belief in oralism was a constant throughout her life and was expressed in numerous works, from the early essay, "My Education in a Convent School for the Deaf," in 1931, to one of her later writings, "Mrs. Spencer Tracy is Right: A Plea for Normal Education for the Deaf," in 1952.

dedication. All of her portraits, whether of deaf people or the institutions of her time, give us a remarkably complete picture of the late nineteenth through the early twentieth centuries.

Rocheleau, with her strong opposition to sign language, would appear to be the most problematical in terms of her relationship with the deaf community. But her attachment to the Montreal Institution for Deaf Girls, to the people there and to its mission, was lifelong, from her days as a student to the time she took up residence in the lay quarters after the death of her husband in 1940. At the school, she continued to do much research and writing in the area of deaf education, including the development of curricula for deaf students. She also worked, in later years, at the Social Services division of the convent. But her connection to the convent school was more than an intellectual one. Even into her later years, she participated in the life of the deaf residents of the convent, sharing in their joys and their sorrows.

These three deaf biographers chose unique people from among the deaf community's leaders to become the heroes of their biographical narratives. Their subjects were not kings or queens, famous poets or artists, or government officials, and, with some exceptions, like Helen Keller, they were not generally known by the community at large. They were individuals who had an intimate connection to the psychology of the biographers and who had generally made a contribution to the deaf and deaf-blind communities.

Berthier offers us the hearing Auguste Bébian, outrageous in the manner in which he opposes an insensitive administration, but admirable in his devotion to his deaf students and their causes. Jean Massieu is presented with his odd quirks, along with a brilliance that impressed both the deaf and the hearing people who knew him; and Laurent Clerc is portrayed as torn between his desire to create a better life for himself in America and his love for his French roots. Berthier creates compelling portraits that certainly gain our interest, but perhaps more importantly, he preserves the lives of men who would have been ignored by hearing biographers, for his heroes were not a part of the hearing world.

Pitrois goes even further than Berthier in chronicling particularly vulnerable heroes, often deaf-blind protagonists. Her story of the little-known but touching Marie Heurtin reveals how, in spite of unpromising beginnings, a deaf-blind child was successfully educated at Notre-Dame de Larnay, the school for the deaf near Poitiers.[8]

Rocheleau similarly presents an unusual heroine, the deaf-blind Ludivine Lachance, who spent thirteen years of her life locked in a closet by an indigent, ignorant family. When sent to the Sisters of Providence at the age of sixteen, she could not eat or move properly and had only the most primitive form of communication. The sisters gave her not only an intellectual, but a spiritual and moral, education that was remarkable in its results, given such a limited point of departure. The Sisters of Providence share the spotlight with Lachance and provide us with an additional layer of heroines. Showing great compassion and wisdom in their work with Lachance, the sisters are dedicated to gaining the skills needed to teach her.

Although these are unexpected heroes, even for authors who had experienced the liberating currents of Romanticism that broadened, to some extent, the definition of the hero and the heroic in nineteenth-century France, they are valuable protagonists. All of the individuals made a contribution to their age, either by performing a valuable social service or by offering those around them an opportunity to develop spiritual generosity and compassion.

These heroes were sustained, as well, by similar social structures. Institutions for the deaf and deaf-blind, by their presence and by their absence, performed an important function in the subjects' and the biographers' lives. Berthier became a student at the National Institute for the Deaf in Paris in 1811 and stayed to serve as a teacher in the same institution, sharing in all of its dramas. In his letters to Désiré Ordinaire, protesting against the rotation system, he spoke of the unique relationship that he and the other deaf instructors had with this institution whose teachers had, in fact, brought him up. In this institution, Berthier learned the best teaching methods, and he bonded with his deaf brothers. Berthier treasured these friendships throughout his life and sought to maintain the cohesiveness of the deaf community by establishing banquets for the deaf community, presenting himself as a candidate for the Constituent Assembly, inspiring an artistic spirit in his deaf countrymen, and commemorating the people who inhabited the Royal Institution and shaped its policies.

Rocheleau had a similar lifelong attachment to one institution, the Montreal Institution for Deaf girls, run by the Sisters of Providence. She was sixteen when she arrived there, but the institution opened up a future for her just as the National Institute had for Berthier. The method through which she learned was oralism, as opposed to the signing that Berthier advocated, but, like him, she developed socially, morally, and intellectually, learning an impressive range of skills. The cooking and general home economics skills enabled her, after the death of her parents, to create a home for two hearing sisters and, later, for her husband, Wilfrid Rouleau. Her literary skills and passion for reading and writing led her to write several impressive biographies that chronicled people and events in both the hearing and deaf worlds. The most famous of them, *Hors de sa prison*, is set in the Montreal school. This biography is more than an inspiring story; it is a love poem to the convent school and its staff for their dedication to their deaf students and for their desire to help them to forge creative, useful lives.

Unlike Berthier and Rocheleau, Pitrois did not discover the deaf community as a student during her early years. Educated by her mother, who did not want to put her daughter into an institution for deaf students, Pitrois's education was a solitary enterprise accomplished in the family home. Pitrois did not meet another deaf person until she was seventeen. At that point, she began to correspond with other deaf individuals and was introduced to the importance and power of the deaf community. She saw herself as uniquely able to provide support, understanding, and moral teaching to her deaf and deaf-blind "little sisters," which she did in her newsletters for them, *La Petite Silencieuse* and *Le Rayon de Soleil*.

Many of the lead articles in these newsletters are portraits of institutions serving the deaf. Pitrois traces their histories and philosophies, including the individuals who founded and inhabited them. In her essay "A Pioneer School in Canada," Pitrois describes the establishment of this French school for deaf boys in 1848 in Canada, through the efforts of the Abbé Lagorce.[9] Lagorce was inspired by a desire to help two deaf boys in his parish. The good abbé gave himself completely to the task and encouraged a nun, Sister Marie de Bon Secours, to do comparable work on behalf of the deaf girls of Montreal. Lagorce is revered as the Abbé de l'Épée of French Canada.

Pitrois ended her article, as she often did, with an appeal for financial aid for the school. She reported that the students came from poor and often uninvolved families. More than half of the 250 families paid nothing to the institution. The Canadian Catholic church largely financed the school, and additional funds came from charitable groups. Pitrois expressed the hope that the government, along with an increase in charitable support, would ensure the continued existence of this fine school.

Pitrois's biographies also included descriptions of the institutions with which her subjects were associated. In *La Vie de l'Abbé de l'Épée racontée aux Sourds-Muets*, Pitrois carefully described the first school for deaf children in France. In her essay on the Heurtin family, which included three deaf-blind children, Pitrois discusses the school for deaf and blind girls in Larnay, France.[10] She provides details of the classrooms, the methods used by the teachers, and the teachers' work and spiritual dedication to their students.

Although Pitrois did not have a close connection to a specific deaf institution that Berthier and Rocheleau had, she developed a deep understanding of the importance of deaf institutions to the moral and intellectual development of deaf individuals. It can, in fact, be argued that she herself became a supportive institution, acting as a social service bureau of one in writing her newsletters for deaf and blind people. Through the newsletters she facilitated the exchange of information, books, gifts, and money to support those most in need and to develop the generosity of those more fortunate. Perhaps there was an unconscious need to offer deaf girls the gift of the deaf community, the one aspect of education and solace that her mother alone was unable to provide.

BERTHIER, PITROIS, and Rocheleau all introduced their readers to the previously unknown world of deaf institutions and the French deaf experience. Nonetheless, all three of them, in time, became known to the larger society in impressive ways. Berthier, who detailed the dramas within the National Institution, knew kings of France and received the cross of the Legion of Honor. Pitrois and Rocheleau bridged the gap even further by writing about hearing people.

Yvonne Pitrois wrote biographies of both famous and relatively unknown hearing people who had led noble and challenging lives. *Ombres de Femmes* (*Shadows of Women*), includes portraits of Victor Hugo's daughter Adèle, Lamartine's mother, and the lesser-known heroic French Lorraine peasant, Suzanne Didier, who was killed by the Germans for refusing to reveal the direction taken by the French army.[11] Pitrois's biography of Abraham Lincoln holds a fascination for both hearing and deaf readers in its portrayal of Lincoln's difficult early years. Pitrois stressed his marginality in terms of the poverty and sadness that alienated him from more fortunate peers for many years.[12] Pitrois was decorated by the King of Belgium for her efforts on behalf of Belgian deaf people during World War I, and she received a medal of honor from the French Welfare Society "for devotion to mankind."[13] Her literary work was similarly recognized, and she was made an officer of the French Academy.

In *Françaises d'Amérique*, Corinne Rocheleau broadened her focus to present the lives of Franco-American women, another group with whom she had a familial and a spiritual connection. She received a gold medal for *Hors de sa prison* from the French Academy and became the first woman to receive the medal of honor from the Franco-American Historical Society of Boston.

Each writer had his or her own style and artistry, and these seem to be more reflective of their individual personalities and educational backgrounds than of their deafness. Berthier's scholarly precision and desire for accuracy and fairness led to impeccable research and writing that was, nonetheless, never dull. On page 11 of his life of the Abbé de l'Épée, Berthier tells us that Father Vanin (or Fanin) taught the deaf sisters before the Abbé de l'Épée assumed responsibility for them. This may be a small matter, but Berthier was unhappy with himself for not knowing the precise spelling of the priest's name. He was equally conscientious about more serious matters and tried to carefully dissect the motives that moved his characters. For example, he offers an array of possibilities—educational, psychological, financial—as to why Laurent Clerc accepted Gallaudet's invitation to come to America with him.

Seemingly unconscious connections between form and content surface in Berthier's biographies, as well. The distressingly short life of Bébian is mirrored by Berthier's truncated narrative. The story ends in a rare, almost complete, loss of objectivity as Berthier mourns the untimely loss of his former mentor and friend. The biography of the Abbé de l'Épée, on the other hand, is unlike Berthier's other work in its distance from the hero and its deification of the abbé. Berthier discussed few faults and depicted L'Epée more as a legend than as a man. The inclusion of an episode in the life of St. Francis, in which he showed great generosity to a deaf servant, reinforces the interpretation of this work as closer to hagiography than biography.

Further examples of a union of form and content can be seen in the studies of Massieu and Clerc appended to the long biography of the Abbé Sicard. This is quite reflective of their situation in life; the two students were, in some sense, appendages to their rather flawed mentor during the years they studied and worked with him.

Pitrois used powerful visual imagery in her narratives. Themes of alternating light and darkness are present in most of her biographies, reflecting the trauma that she experienced when she lost her vision for five years during her childhood. On another level, the imagery also indicates a tension between good and evil, knowledge and ignorance. In

Pitrois's telling of L'Épée's life, the abbé led the deaf sisters from their moral darkness to light by educating them. Anne Sullivan performed that same role when she taught Helen Keller her first word, thus giving Keller the key to human language. Pitrois also created tableaux in her narratives that remain with us long after our reading of her biographies. In the life of the Abbé de l'Épée, we see the mother crying over her two daughters who put their heads on her shoulders, sharing her obvious distress, although they don't understand its origins, while the abbé watches empathically. In the biography of Helen Keller, we remember the dramatic scene in which Helen receives the gift of language. Understanding illuminates her face as water from the well gushes over her hand.

Rocheleau was the most consciously experimental of the three writers with regard to form, and although she certainly had strong moral views, she seemed more dedicated to the notion of art for art's sake than the others. Berthier and Pitrois were also devoted to their craft, but Berthier used his art to deliver a political message, while Pitrois used hers in the service of morality.

In Rocheleau's *Françaises d'Amérique* the narrative point of view shifts from story to story, as does the tone, depending upon the nature of the narrator and the life that she led. Madame Hébert recounted her early life as a settler to her daughter in an emotional, open narrative. The cloistered Jeanne le Ber was such a recluse that she surrendered speech, as belonging to a world outside of the spiritual one she wanted to inhabit in her solitude, and it was her cousin who told her story. Rocheleau's imagery, like that of Pitrois is powerful. The locked door that shuts in Ludivine Lachance in *Hors de sa prison* is gradually replaced in the text by the image of an increasingly liberated Ludivine, climbing freely up the ladder between the courtyard and the convent. The locked door of her mind is similarly opened to new ideas and an impressive level of education, given the family situation in her early years. Rocheleau found the perfect images to signal Ludivine's spiritual transformation.

The intriguing juxtaposition of similarities and differences among

Berthier, Pitrois, and Rocheleau lead us as readers to a wonderful variety of perspectives on art and on life. These three deaf biographers of great intelligence and creativity bridged the gap between themselves and hearing people by using their art to help them resolve personal issues and to depict for readers of their own time and future generations the world in which they lived. They did so with great integrity as moral human beings and as earnest biographers who aspired to convey these stories with accuracy and fidelity to their subjects. In so doing, they left us a legacy that enriches us immeasurably.

Notes

1. On the Nature of Biographical Form

1. André Maurois, *Aspects of Biography*, trans. Sydney Castle Roberts (New York: D. Appleton and Company, 1930), 132.

2. Leon Edel, *Writing Lives: Principia Biographica* (New York: W. W. Norton and Company, 1984), 4.

3. Maurois, *Aspects of Biography*, 109–10.

4. Ibid., 103.

5. I offered a literal rendition of the periodical's title although *The Little Deaf Girl* was another possibility, and might be more reflective of its content and intended audience.

6. Maurois, *Aspects of Biography*, 165.

7. Edel, *Writing Lives*, 26.

8. Ibid., 60.

9. Ibid., 4.

10. Ibid., 151.

11. Ibid., 29.

12. Maurois, *Aspects of Biography*, 134.

13. Ibid., 204.

14. Ibid., 203.

15. G. Thomas Couser, *Recovering Bodies: Illness, Disability and Life Writing* (Madison: University of Wisconsin Press, 1997), 13.

16. Ibid., 230.

17. Ibid., 4.

18. Ibid., 284.

19. Ibid., 295.

2. Crossing the Divide

1. Yvonne Pitrois, *Une nuit rayonnante: Helen Keller* (Neuchatel: A. Delapraz, 1922, 7).

2. Ibid., 9.

3. Ibid., 11.

4. Ibid., 58.

5. Ibid., 59.

6. Helen Keller, letter to Yvonne Pitrois, n.d., Collections of the American Foundation for the Blind, New York City, 1.

7. Ibid.

8. Ibid., 5.

9. Script, Mrs. [Sullivan] Macy and Helen Keller in Vaudeville, n.d., Vaudeville File, Collections of the American Foundation for the Blind, New York City, 5.

10. Questions Asked Helen Keller by Her Vaudeville Audience, n.d., Vaudeville File, Collections of the American Foundation for the Blind, New York City.

11. Helen Keller, letter to Daisy Sharpe, December 19, 1923, Vaudeville File, Collections of the American Foundation for the Blind, New York City.

12. Dorothy Herrmann, *Helen Keller, A Life* (New York: Alfred A. Knopf, 1998) 213.

13. Ibid., 223.

14. *Keith's Theatre News* (Washington) May 24, 1920: 3.

15. E. Drouot, "Un auteur sourd," *Revue Générale de l'Enseignement des Sourds-Muets* 14 annee-n 5 (1912): 97–99.

16. Keller, letter to Yvonne Pitrois, 2.

3. Jean-Ferdinand Berthier

1. Armand Pelletier, préface, *Aux Origines du Mouvement Sourd Ferdinand Berthier,1803–1886* , ed. Yves Delaporte (Louhans: CLSFB, 1999), 3.

2. Christian Cuxac, "Le Congrès de Milan," in *Le Pouvoir des Signes*, ed. Lysiane Couturier and Alexis Karacostas (Paris: Imprimerie Borel, 1989), 100.

3. Cuxac, "Le Congrès de Milan," 102–6.

4. Pelletier, preface, *Aux Origines du Mouvement Sourd*, 3.

5. Yves Delaporte, ed., *Aux Origines du Mouvement Sourd Ferdinand Berthier, 1803–1886* (Louhans: CLSFB, 1999) 4.

6. Ibid., 39.

7. Ibid., 44.

8. Ibid., 60.

9. Ibid., 15.

10. Ibid., 25–29.

11. Ibid., 76.

12. Bernard Mottez, "Les Banquets de Sourds-Muets et la Naissance du Mouvement Sourd," in *Le Pouvoir des Signes*, ed. Lysiane Couturier and Alexis Karacostas (Paris: Imprimerie Borel, 1989), 170.

13. Delaporte, *Aux Origines du Mouvement Sourd*, 82.

14. Ibid., 16.

15. Ibid., 36.

16. Ferdinand Berthier, *Notice sur la Vie et les Ouvrages d'Auguste Bébian, Ancien Censeur des Études de l'Institut Royal des Sourds-Muets de Paris* (Paris: J. Ledoyen, 1839).

17. Ibid., 21.

18. Ibid., 23–24.

19. Ibid., 24.

20. Ferdinand Berthier, *L'Abbé de l'Épée, Sa Vie, Son Apostolat, Ses Travaux, Sa Lutte et Ses Succès; avec l'Historique des Monuments Élevés à Sa Mémoire à Paris et à Versailles* (Paris: Michel Lévy Frères, 1852), 8.

21. Alexis Karacostas, "L'Abbé de l'Épée: Un 'Bienfaiteur de l'Humanité'," *Le Pouvoir des Signes*, ed. Lysiane Couturier and Alexis Karacostas (Paris: Imprimerie Borel, 1999), 33.

22. Berthier, *L'Abbé de l'Épée*, 10.

23. Karacostas, "L'Abbé de l'Épée ," 33.

24. Berthier, *L'Abbé de l'Épée*, 50.

25. Ferdinand Berthier, *L'Abbé Sicard, Précis Historique sur Sa Vie, Ses Travaux et Ses Succès; suivi de détails biographiques sur ses élèves sourds-muets les plus remarquables, Jean Massieu et Laurent Clerc, et d'un appendice contenant des lettres de l'abbé Sicard au baron de Gérando* (Paris: Charles Douniol et Cie, 1873).

26. Ibid., 19.

27. Ibid., 50.

28. Ibid., 117.

29. Ibid., 143.

30. Ibid., 146–47.

31. Ibid., 150.

32. Ibid., 154.

33. Ibid., 162.

34. Alexis Karacostas, "De l'Ombre à la Lumière: les Sourds et la Révolution Française," *Le Pouvoir des Signes*, ed. Lysiane Couturier and Alexis Karacostas (Paris: Imprimerie Borel, 1999), 62.

35. Harlan Lane, "Les Sourds aux États-Unis après Laurent Clerc," *Le Pouvoir des Signes*, ed. Lysiane Couturier and Alexis Karacostas (Paris: Imprimerie Borel, 1989), 215.

36. Berthier, *L'Abbé Sicard*, 186.

37. Lane, "Les Sourds aux États-Unis," 216.

38. Ibid., 216.

39. Berthier, *L'Abbé Sicard*, 187.

40. Ibid., 190.

4. Yvonne Pitrois

1. H. Montague, "Yvonne Pitrois," *Volta Review* 39 (1937):409.

2. E. Florence Long, "Mlle Yvonne Pitrois," *Ephpheta* 6 (1917):5.

3. Guilbert C. Braddock, *Notable Deaf Persons*, ed. Florence B. Crammatte (Washington, DC: Gallaudet College Alumni Association, 1975), 198.

4. E. Drouot, "Un auteur sourd," *Revue Générale de l'Enseignement des Sourds-Muets*, year 14, no. 5 (1912):97–98.

5. Ibid., 98.

6. Ibid.

7. Ibid.

8. Yvonne Pitrois, *Bernard Palissy* (Strasbourg: Éditions Oberlin, n.d.).3.

9. Pitrois, *Bernard Palissy*, 26.

10. Drouot, 98.

11. Montague, "Yvonne Pitrois," 421.

12. Yvonne Pitrois, *Une Humble Vie ou Comment Puis-Je Lui Faire Du Bien* (Strasbourg: Librairie Évangélique, 1929), 30.

13. Braddock, *Notable Deaf Persons*, 198–99.

14. Yvonne Pitrois, *La Vie de l'Abbé de l'Épée Racontée aux Sourds-Muets* (Saint-Étienne: Imprimerie de l'Institution des Sourds-Muets, 1912), 6.

15. Ibid., 9.

16. Ibid., 12.

17. Ibid., 15.

18. Ibid., 17.

19. Pitrois, *La Vie de l'Abbé de l'Épée*, 29.

20. Yvonne Pitrois, "Une humble Chrétienne," *La Petite Silencieuse*, year 1, no. 5 (1913): 41–43.

21. M. L. Hance, "Yvonne Pitrois," *Volta Review* 30 (1928):361.

22. Yvonne Pitrois, "Nouvelles de nos Sourdes-Muettes-Aveugles," *La Petite Silencieuse*, year 1, no. 3 (1913): 30–31.

23. Hance, "Yvonne Pitrois," 361.

24. Yvonne Pitrois, *Lettre d'une Française à Nos Soldats* (Paris: A. Rasquin, 1918), 1–2.

25. Yvonne Pitrois, "A Deaf-Blind Hero of France," *Silent Worker* 37 (1925): 165–68.

26. Braddock, *Notable Deaf Persons*, 199.

27. Yvonne Pitrois, "A School for the Deaf in Montreal," *Volta Review* 37 (1935): 406–7.

28. Yvonne Pitrois, "The Heurtin Family," *Volta Review* 12 (1911):733–48.

29. Yvonne Pitrois, *Sourds-Muets-Aveugles* (Strasbourg: Librairie Évangélique, 1929), 17–20.

30. Pitrois, *Sourds-Muets-Aveugles*, 19.

31. Yvonne Pitrois, "Madame Marguerite Pitrois," *La Petite Silencieuse*, year 14, no. 6 (1926):1–3.

32. Pitrois, "Madame Marguerite Pitrois," 2.

33. Montague, "Yvonne Pitrois," 409.

34. Ibid., 421.

5. *Corinne Rocheleau*

1. Leon Edel, *Writing Lives: Principia Biographica* (New York: W. W. Norton, 1984), 4.

2. Ibid., 65, 68.

3. Yvonne Pitrois, "Corinne Rocheleau: The Author of *Out of Her Prison*," *Volta Review* 21.3 (Jan. 1929):5.

4. Ibid., 5.

5. Corinne Rocheleau-Rouleau, "My Education in a Convent School for the Deaf," *Catholic Educational Review* 29 (1931):267.

6. Ibid.

7. Ibid., 269.

8. Ibid., 270.

9. Ibid., 271.

10. Ibid., 271.

11. Ibid., 273.

12. Ibid., 276.

13. Rosaire Dion-Lévesque, *Silhouettes Franco-Américaines* (Manchester, N.H.: Ballard Frères, 1957), 783.

14. Rocheleau-Rouleau, "My Education," 277.

15. Couser, *Recovering Bodies*, 222.

16. Rocheleau-Rouleau, "My Education," 278.

17. Heilbrun, *Women's Lives*, 68.

18. Pitrois, "Corinne Rocheleau," 6.

19. André Maurois, *Aspects of Biography*, trans. Sydney Castle Roberts (New York: D. Appleton and Company, 1930), 125.

20. Corinne Rocheleau-Rouleau, *Françaises d'Amérique: Esquisse historique. Quelques traits vécus de la vie des principales héroïnes de la Nouvelle-France* (Worcester: La Compagnie de Publication Belisle, 1915), 16.

21. Couser, *Recovering Bodies*, 288.

22. Ibid., 295.

23. Heilbrun, *Women's Lives*, 66–67.

24. Carol Padden and Tom Humphries, *Deaf in America: Voices from a Culture* (Cambridge: Harvard University Press, 1988), 111.

25. Rocheleau-Rouleau, "My Education," 267.

6. Biography in Deaf Hands

1. Jean-Ferdinand Berthier, *Notice sur la Vie et les Ouvrages d'Auguste Bébian, Ancien Censeur des Études de l'Institut Royal des Sourds-Muets de Paris* (Paris: Ledoyen,1839), 46.

2. Jean-Ferdinand Berthier, *L'Abbé de l'Épée, Sa Vie, Son Apostolat, Ses Travaux, Ses Succès avec l'Historique des Monuments Élevés à Sa Mémoire à Paris et à Versailles* (Paris: Michel Lévy Frères, 1852), 10.

3. Margaret Hance, "Yvonne Pitrois," *Volta Review* 30 (July 1928):360–62.

4. Ibid., 361.

5. Ibid.

6. Yvonne Pitrois, "Marguerite Pitrois," *La Petite Silencieuse* (Nov.–Déc. 1926):2–3.

7. Yvonne Pitrois, "The National Institution for the Deaf in Paris," *Volta Review* 14 (March 1913): 710–18.

8. Yvonne Pitrois, *Sourds-Muets-Aveugles!* (Strasbourg:Librairie Évangélique, 1929), 14–23.

9. Yvonne Pitrois, "A Pioneer School in Canada," *Volta Review* 38 (Jan. 1936):22.

10. Yvonne Pitrois, "The Heurtin Family," *Volta Review* 12 (March 1911):733–48.

11. Yvonne Pitrois, *Ombres de Femmes* (Lausanne-Genève-Neuchâtel-Vevey-Montreux-Berne: Librairie Payot et Compagnie, 1925).

12. Yvonne Pitrois, *Abraham Lincoln le libérateur des esclaves* (Toulouse: Société d'Édition de Toulouse, 1912).

13. Hance, "Yvonne Pitrois," 361.

Bibliography

Published Sources

America, a Record of Today. Washington, D.C.: Volta Bureau, 1930.

Bellerive, Georges. *Nos auteurs dramatiques anciens et contemporains. Répertoire analytique*. Montréal: Beauchemin,1933.

Berthier, Ferdinand. *L'Abbé de l'Épée, sa vie, son apostolat, ses travaux et ses succès avec l'historique des monuments élevés à sa mémoire à Paris et à Versailles*. Paris: Michel Lévy Frères, 1852.

———. *L'Abbé Sicard, précis historique de sa vie, ses travaux, ses succès, suivis de détails biographiques sur ses élèves les plus remarquables, Jean Massieu et Laurent Clerc, et d'un appendice contenant des lettres de l'abbé Sicard au baron de Gérando*. Paris: C. Douniol, 1873.

———. *Un Mot sur le Buste de l'Abbé de l'Épée à l'Église Saint Roch, à Paris, et Sa Statue à Versailles*. Paris: Donnaud, 1874.

———. *Notice sur la vie et les ouvrages d'Auguste Bébian, ancien censeur des études de l'Institut Royal des Sourds-Muets de Paris*. Paris: J. Ledoyen, 1839.

Bitard, A. "Jean-Ferdinand Berthier." *Dictionnaire Général de Biographie Contemporaine*. 1878. 168–69.

Braddock, Guilbert C. *Notable Deaf Persons*. Edited by Florence B. Crammatte. Washington, DC: Gallaudet College Alumni Association, 1975.

Brooks, Van Wyck. *Helen Keller. Sketch for a Portrait*. New York: E. P. Dutton and Co. Inc., 1956.

Couser, G. Thomas. *Recovering Bodies: Illness, Disability and Life Writing*. Madison: University of Wisconsin Press, 1997.

Cuxac, Christian. "Le Congrès de Milan." In *Le Pouvoir des Signes*, edited by Lysiane Couturier and Alexis Karacostas, 76–83. Paris: Borel, 1989.

Delaporte, Yves, éd. *Aux Origines du Mouvement Sourd: Ferdinand Berthier, 1803–1886*. Louhans: CLSFB, 1999.

Dion-Lévesque, Rosaire. *Silhouettes Franco-Américaines*. Manchester, New Hampshire: Ballard Frères, 1957.

Drouot, E. "Un auteur sourd." *Revue Générale de l'Enseignement des Sourds-Muets* 14, no. 5 (1912):97–99.

Edel, Leon. *Writing Lives: Principia Biographica*. New York: W. W. Norton and Company, 1984.

Forestier, Claudius. *Parallèle entre l'Instruction des Sourds-Muets par le Lan-*

gage des Signes et Leur Enseignement par l'Articulation Artificielle. Lyon: Pitrat aîné, 1883.

Freeberg, Ernest. *The Education of Laura Bridgman: First Deaf and Blind Person to Learn Language*. Cambridge: Harvard University Press, 2000.

Gibson, William. *The Miracle Worker*. New York: Bantam Books, 1975.

Gitter, Elisabeth. *The Imprisoned Guest: Samuel Howe and Laura Bridgman, the Original Deaf-Blind Girl*. New York: Farrar, Straus and Giroux, 2001.

Glaeser, E. "Jean-Ferdinand Berthier." In *Biographie Nationale des Contemporains*, 170–73. 1878.

Golladay, L. "Yvonne Pitrois." In *Gallaudet Encyclopedia of Deaf People and Deafness*, edited by J. V. Van Cleve., vol. 2, 294–95. New York: McGraw-Hill, 1987.

Hance, M. L. "Yvonne Pitrois." *Volta Review* 30 (July 1928):360–62.

Heilbrun, Carolyn. *Women's Lives: The View from the Threshold*. Toronto: University of Toronto Press, 1999.

Herrmann, Dorothy. *Helen Keller, A Life*. New York: Alfred A. Knopf, 1998.

Karacostas, Alexis. "L'Abbé de l'Épée, un 'Bienfaiteur de l'Humanité'." In *Le Pouvoir des Signes*, edited by Lysiane Couturier and Alexis Karacostas, 33. Paris: Borel, 1989.

———. "De l'Ombre à la Lumière: Les Sourds et la Révolution Française." In *Le Pouvoir des Signes*, edited by Lysiane Couturier and Alexis Karacostas, 60–68. Paris: Borel, 1989.

Keith's Theatre News (Washington, DC). May 24, 1920:1ff.

Keller, Helen. "Hommage d'Helen Keller à l'Abbé de l'Épée." *Revue Générale de l'Enseignement des Sourds-Muets* 14, no. 4 (1912):80–82.

———. *The Story of My Life*. New York: Bantam, 1990.

Lane, Harlan. "Les Sourds aux États-Unis après Laurent Clerc." In *Le Pouvoir des Signes*, edited by Lysiane Couturier and Alexis Karacostas, 215–25. Paris: Borel, 1989.

Lang, Harry G., and Bonnie Meath-Lang. *Deaf Persons in the Arts and Sciences*. Westport, CT: Greenwood Press, 1995.

Lash, Joseph P. *Helen and Teacher: The Story of Helen Keller and Anne Sullivan Macy*. New York: Delacorte Press, 1980.

Letters of Jean-Ferdinand Berthier, 1834–1836. Archives of the Institut National de Jeunes Sourds, Paris, France.

Long, E. Florence. "Mlle Yvonne Pitrois." *Ephpheta* 6 (1917):5–6.

Maurois, André. *Aspects of Biography*. Translated by Sydney Castle Roberts. New York: D. Appleton and Company, 1930.

Montague, H. "Yvonne Pitrois." *Volta Review* 39 (1937): 409–421.

Moody, William. "Jean-Ferdinand Berthier." In *Gallaudet Encyclopedia of Deaf People and Deafness*, edited by John Van Cleve, in vol. 1. New York: McGraw-Hill Book Company, Inc., 1987.

Mottez, Bernard. "Les Banquets de Sourds-Muets et la Naissance du Mouvement Sourd." In *Le Pouvoir des Signes*, edited by Lysiane Couturier et Alexis Karacostas, 170–77. Paris: Borel, 1989.

Padden, Carol, and Tom Humphries. *Deaf in America: Voices from a Culture.* Cambridge: Harvard University Press, 1988.

Pelletier, Armand, ed. *Ferdinand Berthier, Sourd, Professeur, Écrivain, Militant, Chevalier de la Légion d'Honneur.* Louhans: CLSFB, 1996.

Pitrois, Yvonne. *Abraham Lincoln le libérateur des esclaves.* Toulouse: Société d'Édition de Toulouse, 1912.

———. *Bernard Palissy.* Strasbourg: Éditions Oberlin, n.d.

———. "Corinne Rocheleau: The Author of *Out of Her Prison.*" *Volta Review* 21.3 (Jan. 1929):5–7.

———. "A Deaf-Blind Hero of France." *The Silent Worker* 37 (1925):165–68.

———. "The Heurtin Family." *Volta Review* 12 (Mar. 1911):733–48.

———. "Une humble Chrétienne." *La Petite Silencieuse* première année numéro 5 (1913):41–43.

———. *Une Humble Vie ou Comment Puis-Je Lui Faire Du Bien?* Strasbourg: Librairie Évangélique, 1929.

———. "L'Institution Nationale de Sourdes-Muettes de Bordeaux." *La Petite Silencieuse* première année numéro 2 (1913):15–17.

———. "Les Larmes d'une Mère." *La Petite Silencieuse,* year 1, no. 3 (1913):21–22.

———. *Lettre d'une Française à Nos Soldats.* Paris: A. Rasquin, 1918.

———. "Madame Marguerite G. Pitrois." *La Petite Silencieuse* 14, no. 6 (1926): 1–3.

———. "The National Institution for the Deaf in Paris." *Volta Review* 14 (Mar. 1913):710–18.

———. "Nouvelles de Nos Sourdes-Muettes-Aveugles: Helen Keller." *La Petite Silencieuse* 1, no. 3 (1913):31.

———. *Une nuit rayonnante: Helen Keller.* Neuchâtel: A Delapraz, 1922.

———. *Ombres de Femmes.* Lausanne: Librairie Payot et Compagnie, 1925.

———. "*Out of Her Prison:* The Pathetic Story of Ludivine Lachance." *Volta Review* 30.12 (Dec. 1928):783–87.

———. "A Pioneer School in Canada." *Volta Review* 38 (1936): 22.

———. "A School for the Deaf in Montreal." *Volta Review* 37 (1935):406–7.

———. *Sourds-Muets-Aveugles.* Strasbourg: Librairie Évangelique, 1929

———. *Trois Lumières dans la Nuit: Valentin Haüy, Louis Braille, Maurice de la Sizeranne.* Strasbourg: Imprimerie de la Petite France, 1936.

———. *La Vie de l'Abbé de l'Épée Racontée aux Sourds-Muets.* Saint-Étienne: Imprimerie de l'Institution des Sourds-Muets, 1912.

Quartararo, Anne. "The Life and Times of Ferdinand Berthier: A Historical Analysis." Presented at the Fourth Deaf History International Conference, Gallaudet University, Summer 2000.

Rocheleau, Corinne. *Françaises d'Amérique: Esquisse Historique (Quelques traits vécus de la vie des principales héroïnes de la Nouvelle France)*. Worcester: La Compagnie de Publication Belisle, 1915.

———— *Hors de sa prison: Extraordinaire histoire de Ludivine Lachance l'infirme des infirmes, sourde, muette et aveugle*. Montréal: Imprimerie Arbour et Dupont, 1927.

———. "Mrs. Spencer Tracy Is Right. A Plea for Normal Education of the Deaf." Article, ts. Archives of L'Institution des Sourdes-Muettes, Montreal, March 1952.

———. "My Education in a Convent School for the Deaf." *Catholic Educational Review* 29 (1931):266–82.

Rocheleau, Corinne, with Rebecca Mack. *Those in the Dark Silence, the Deaf-Blind in North America, a Record of Today*. Washington, D.C.: The Volta Bureau, 1930.

Unpublished Sources

Keller, Helen. Letter to Daisy Sharpe. December 19, 1923. Collections of the American Foundation for the Blind, New York City.

———. Letter to Yvonne Pitrois. n.d. Collections of the American Foundation for the Blind, New York City.

Questions asked Helen Keller by Her Vaudeville Audience. n.d. Vaudeville File. Collections of the American Foundation for the Blind.

Script. Mrs. [Sullivan] Macy and Helen Keller in Vaudeville. n.d. Vaudeville File. Collections of the American Foundation for the Blind.

Index